A Vers de Société

Compiler: Carolyn Wells

Alpha Editions

This edition published in 2024

ISBN : 9789362926692

Design and Setting By
Alpha Editions
www.alphaedis.com
Email - info@alphaedis.com

As per information held with us this book is in Public Domain.
This book is a reproduction of an important historical work. Alpha Editions uses the best technology to reproduce historical work in the same manner it was first published to preserve its original nature. Any marks or number seen are left intentionally to preserve its true form.

Contents

NOTE	- 1 -
INTRODUCTION	- 2 -
TO CELIA	- 6 -
CUPID	- 7 -
ROSALIND'S MADRIGAL	- 9 -
ALL THINGS EXCEPT MYSELF I KNOW	- 11 -
CUPID AND CAMPASPE	- 13 -
A DITTY	- 14 -
SONG FROM "TWELFTH NIGHT"	- 15 -
SIGH NO MORE (From *"Much Ado About Nothing"*)	- 16 -
PHILLIDA AND CORYDON	- 17 -
CHERRY-RIPE	- 19 -
SEND BACK MY LONG-STRAY'D EYES TO ME	- 20 -
PACK CLOUDS AWAY	- 21 -
SHALL I, WASTING IN DESPAIR	- 22 -
TO THE VIRGINS TO MAKE MUCH OF TIME	- 24 -
THE BRACELET	- 25 -
AN OLD RHYME	- 26 -
LOVE ME NOT FOR COMELY GRACE	- 27 -
ON A GIRDLE	- 28 -
TO MY LOVE	- 29 -
TO ALTHEA (FROM PRISON)	- 30 -
SONG	- 32 -
THE DESPAIRING LOVER	- 33 -
CUPID MISTAKEN	- 35 -
THE CONTRAST	- 36 -

OH, TELL ME HOW TO WOO THEE	- 39 -
SONG FROM "THE DUENNA"	- 41 -
THE RACES A BALLAD	- 42 -
TO LADY ANNE HAMILTON	- 45 -
TO MRS. LEIGH UPON HER WEDDING-DAY	- 46 -
NAMES	- 47 -
THE EXCHANGE	- 48 -
DEFIANCE	- 49 -
HER LIPS	- 50 -
COMMINATION	- 51 -
MARGARET AND DORA	- 52 -
A CERTAIN YOUNG LADY	- 53 -
SONG	- 55 -
THE TIME I'VE LOST IN WOOING	- 56 -
WHEN I LOVED YOU	- 58 -
REASON, FOLLY, AND BEAUTY	- 59 -
TIRESOME SPRING!	- 61 -
ROSETTE	- 62 -
SHE IS SO PRETTY	- 63 -
RONDEAU	- 64 -
STOLEN FRUIT	- 65 -
LOVE AND AGE	- 66 -
CLUBS	- 69 -
TO ANNE	- 71 -
SONG	- 72 -
WHAT IS LONDON'S LAST NEW LION?	- 74 -
I'D BE A BUTTERFLY	- 75 -
"I MUST COME OUT NEXT SPRING"	- 76 -

"WHY DON'T THE MEN PROPOSE?"	- 78 -
ASK AND HAVE	- 80 -
LINES IN A YOUNG LADY'S ALBUM	- 81 -
THE TIME OF ROSES	- 83 -
LOVE	- 84 -
TO HELEN	- 85 -
THE BELLE OF THE BALL-ROOM	- 86 -
AMY'S CRUELTY	- 90 -
BEWARE!	- 92 -
LOVE IN A COTTAGE	- 94 -
BECAUSE	- 96 -
LILIAN	- 98 -
THE HENCHMAN	- 100 -
DOROTHY Q A FAMILY PORTRAIT	- 102 -
A REMINISCENCE	- 105 -
THE AGE OF WISDOM	- 106 -
THE BALLAD OF BOUILLABAISSE	- 108 -
AN INVITATION	- 112 -
FANNY; OR THE BEAUTY AND THE BEE	- 114 -
GARDEN FANCIES THE FLOWER'S NAME	- 115 -
A POEM OF EVERY-DAY LIFE	- 118 -
LOVE DISPOSED OF	- 121 -
MABEL, IN NEW HAMPSHIRE	- 123 -
THE COQUETTE A PORTRAIT	- 124 -
JUSTINE, YOU LOVE ME NOT!	- 126 -
SING HEIGH-HO!	- 128 -
SNOWDROP	- 129 -
THE PROTEST	- 130 -

SCHERZO	- 131 -
THE HANDSOMEST MAN IN THE ROOM	- 132 -
THE LAWYER'S INVOCATION TO SPRING	- 134 -
A TERRIBLE INFANT	- 135 -
LOULOU AND HER CAT	- 136 -
PICCADILLY	- 138 -
A WORD THAT MAKES US LINGER	- 140 -
MY MISTRESS'S BOOTS	- 141 -
A NICE CORRESPONDENT!	- 143 -
THERE'S A TIME TO BE JOLLY	- 146 -
I REMEMBER, I REMEMBER	- 147 -
THE FLOWER OF LOVE LIES BLEEDING	- 149 -
THE GOLD ROOM AN IDYL	- 151 -
COMFORT	- 153 -
A SUMMER SONG	- 154 -
MY AUNT'S SPECTRE	- 155 -
A CONCEIT	- 157 -
MARTIAL IN LONDON	- 158 -
THE BEST OF THE BALL	- 159 -
THE BALLAD OF DEAD LADIES	- 161 -
FEMININE ARITHMETIC	- 163 -
A TRIFLE	- 164 -
FLIGHT	- 165 -
LOVE	- 168 -
SINCE WE PARTED	- 170 -
A KISS—BY MISTAKE	- 171 -
A GAME OF FIVES	- 173 -
A VALENTINE	- 174 -

THE WEDDING DAY	- 176 -
EDGED TOOLS	- 178 -
WITCHCRAFT	- 180 -
TOUJOURS AMOUR	- 182 -
DICTUM SAPIENTI	- 184 -
UNDOWERED	- 185 -
THE LOVE-KNOT	- 186 -
VERS DE SOCIÉTÉ	- 188 -
A LETTER OF ADVICE	- 190 -
AT THE LATTICE	- 192 -
FRENCH WITH A MASTER	- 194 -
ON AN INTAGLIO HEAD OF MINERVA	- 196 -
THE LUNCH	- 198 -
THE WITCH IN THE GLASS	- 199 -
TO PHŒBE	- 200 -
MY LOVE AND MY HEART	- 201 -
TO A COUNTRY COUSIN	- 203 -
THE FAMILY FOOL	- 205 -
AN INTERLUDE	- 208 -
A MATCH	- 211 -
CAPRICE	- 213 -
THE MINUET	- 215 -
A STREET SKETCH	- 217 -
SAINT MAY A CITY LYRIC	- 218 -
PET'S PUNISHMENT	- 220 -
HER LETTER	- 221 -
AVICE	- 224 -
A SONG OF THE FOUR SEASONS	- 227 -

IN TOWN	- 229 -
WHEN I SAW YOU LAST, ROSE	- 231 -
TO "LYDIA LANGUISH"	- 232 -
THE OLD SEDAN CHAIR	- 235 -
"LE ROMAN DE LA ROSE"	- 237 -
NINETY-NINE IN THE SHADE	- 239 -
BRIGHTON PIER	- 240 -
A CONTRADICTION	- 242 -
RONDEL	- 244 -
WHITE, PILLARED NECK	- 245 -
JANET	- 246 -
FOR A FAN	- 247 -
BALLADE OF SUMMER	- 248 -
COLINETTE	- 250 -
BALLADE OF DEAD LADIES (*After Villon*)	- 252 -
IL BACIO	- 254 -
SUR L'HERBE	- 255 -
THE ROMANCE OF A GLOVE	- 256 -
IF	- 258 -
DON'T	- 259 -
ON REREADING TÉLÉMAQUE	- 260 -
VALENTINE	- 261 -
BIFTEK AUX CHAMPIGNONS	- 262 -
AN EXPLANATION	- 265 -
MARJORIE'S KISSES	- 266 -
MISS NANCY'S GOWN	- 267 -
"LE DERNIER JOUR D'UN CONDAMNÉ"	- 269 -
MY WOOING	- 271 -

WINTRY PARIS	- 274 -
THE ROSE	- 275 -
INDECISION	- 276 -
LOGIC	- 277 -
CONVERSATIONAL	- 279 -
IF YOU WANT A KISS, WHY, TAKE IT	- 280 -
EDUCATIONAL COURTSHIP	- 282 -
KISSING'S NO SIN	- 283 -
THE BEST THING IN THE WORLD	- 284 -
HER NEIGHBOURS	- 285 -
TO CELIA	- 286 -
IN FOR IT	- 287 -
KIRTLE RED	- 289 -
A BAGATELLE	- 290 -
A LOVE TEST	- 291 -
THE MISTAKEN MOTH	- 292 -
MY PRETTY NEIGHBOR	- 293 -
IF	- 294 -
TO MISTRESS PYRRHA	- 295 -
THE TEA-GOWN	- 296 -
A PARAPHRASE	- 298 -
A LEAP-YEAR EPISODE	- 299 -
BALLADE OF LADIES' NAMES	- 301 -
BALLADE OF JUNE	- 303 -
BALLADE MADE IN THE HOT WEATHER	- 305 -
A ROSE	- 307 -
TO MINNIE	- 308 -
AN AMERICAN GIRL	- 309 -

LARKS AND NIGHTINGALES	- 311 -
CAELI	- 313 -
LADY MINE	- 314 -
THE RIPEST PEACH[A]	- 315 -
"I JOURNEYED SOUTH TO MEET THE SPRING"	- 316 -
BEFORE THE BLOSSOM	- 317 -
LOVE IN THE CALENDAR	- 318 -
MY GRANDMOTHER'S TURKEY-TAIL FAN	- 320 -
VALENTINE	- 322 -
A VALENTINE	- 324 -
ON A HYMN-BOOK	- 325 -
THE BALLADE OF THE SUMMER-BOARDER	- 327 -
INTERESTING	- 329 -
THE WAY TO ARCADY	- 331 -
DA CAPO	- 335 -
THE MAID OF MURRAY HILL	- 337 -
KITTY'S SUMMERING	- 339 -
FORFEITS	- 340 -
WHEN WILL LOVE COME?	- 341 -
HELIOTROPE	- 342 -
BORDERLAND	- 345 -
EPITHALAMIUM	- 347 -
INFIRM	- 350 -
WORDS, WORDS, WORDS	- 351 -
THE BLUEBELL	- 352 -
A MODERN MARTYRDOM	- 353 -
A CORSAGE BOUQUET	- 356 -
THE BALLAD OF CASSANDRA BROWN	- 357 -

FROM THREE FLY LEAVES	- 359 -
QUESTION AND ANSWER	- 360 -
A RHYME FOR PRISCILLA	- 362 -
THE OLD COLLECTOR	- 365 -
THE LAST DITCH	- 368 -
BE YE IN LOVE WITH APRIL-TIDE	- 370 -
STRAWBERRIES	- 371 -
APPLIED ASTRONOMY	- 372 -
COURTSHIP	- 374 -
EYES OF BLACK AND EYES OF BLUE	- 376 -
HER FAULTS	- 378 -
A MODERN DIALOGUE	- 380 -
THE POET'S PROPOSAL	- 383 -
TRUTH	- 384 -
THE BACHELOR GIRL	- 385 -
THE SEA	- 387 -
IN PHILISTIA	- 388 -
BETWEEN THE SHOWERS	- 390 -
GRACE'S CHOICE	- 391 -
TO VIOLET	- 393 -
HER BONNET	- 394 -
A SONG	- 395 -
LES PAPILLOTTES	- 396 -
UPON GRACIOSA, WALKING AND TALKING	- 398 -
HER VALENTINE	- 399 -
STORY OF THE GATE	- 402 -
TWO TRIOLETS	- 404 -
A BALLADE OF OLD SWEETHEARTS	- 405 -

AMOUR DE VOYAGE	- 407 -
THE LOVERS' LITANY	- 408 -
A LENTEN CALL	- 410 -
HELEN'S FACE A BOOK	- 412 -
THE BUTTERFLY'S MADRIGAL	- 413 -
BALLADE OF THE DEVIL-MAY-CARE	- 414 -
BALLADE OF DREAMS TRANSPOSED	- 416 -
VILLANELLE OF HIS LADY'S TREASURE	- 418 -
L'ENVOI	- 419 -
A MERRY BLUE-EYED LADDIE	- 420 -
DANCE TIME	- 421 -
HOW LIKE A WOMAN	- 423 -
A VIGNETTE	- 424 -

NOTE

ACKNOWLEDGMENT is hereby gratefully made to the publishers for permission to use poems by the following authors:

To Messrs. Houghton, Mifflin and Company for poems by Thomas Bailey Aldrich, Oliver Wendell Holmes, James Russell Lowell, John Greenleaf Whittier, Bret Harte, John G. Saxe, Norah Perry, Henry Wadsworth Longfellow, James T. Field, Edith Thomas, Edmund Clarence Stedman and Charles Henry Webb.

To Messrs. Dodd, Mead and Company for poems by Austin Dobson.

To the Macmillan Company for poems by Lewis Carroll.

To Messrs. D. Appleton and Company for "Song," by William Cullen Bryant.

To The Century Company for poems by Robert Underwood Johnson and Mary Mapes Dodge.

To Messrs. Little, Brown and Company for "A Valentine," by Mrs. Laura E. Richards, and "Shadows" and "Les Papillottes," by Gertrude Hall.

To Messrs. G. P. Putnam's Sons for "The Debutante," by Guy Wetmore Carryl.

To The Frederick A. Stokes Company for poems by Frank Dempster Sherman and Samuel Minturn Peck.

To The Lothrop, Lee and Shepard Company for poems by Sam Walter Foss.

To Messrs. E. H. Bacon and Company for poems by James Jeffrey Roche.

INTRODUCTION

ALL collectors of *Vers de Société* agree that there is no possibility of an English equivalent for the French term. None exists; and the attempts to coin one have invariably resulted in failure.

Society Verse, Familiar Verse and Occasional Verse are all wide of the mark in one direction or another; and perhaps, after all, the simple term Light Verse strikes nearest home.

One might suggest Gentle Verse, but it would be with the restricted meaning of the adjective that is applied to the courteous and well-bred; the innately fine, polished by the experience and sophistication of truly good society.

Gentlefolk are never excessive. Their enthusiasms are modified, their emotions are restrained, their humor is delicate. As a result of wise and intelligent culture, their tastes are refined, their fashions correct. They breathe the air of polite worldly wisdom, which endows them with a gracious ease, and removes all trace of self-consciousness.

D'Israeli says, "Genius is not always sufficient to impart that grace of amenity which seems peculiar to those who are accustomed to elegant society."

Gentle Verse then, would imply lines written of the gentlefolk, for the gentlefolk, and by gentlefolk.

Society Verse is an inadequate term, because Society has come to include both the gentle folk and the others.

Familiar Verse, though staunchly defended by one of our foremost men of letters, allows a latitude of informality that is too liberal for a precise equivalent. Occasional Verse is ambiguous, and Easy Verse, absurd.

Lyra Elegantiarum is an adequate translation, but not into English. And none of the graceful titles yet chosen by our modern poets from "Brightsome Balladry" to "*Lingerie de Poesie*" has as yet fulfilled all requirements.

Granting then that there is no perfect English translation of the French phrase, and accepting *Vers de Société* as our field, we are again confronted by great difficulties and embarrassments in defining its boundaries.

One of the greatest masters of the art, Mr. Austin Dobson, gives us twelve definite rules for our guidance; but of these, only three refer to the matter of the poems, the others being advice as to manner.

Though manner is equally important, yet the choice of matter for *Vers de Société* depends upon certain definite characteristics.

But to limit these characteristics is to ask the question, "who shall decide when doctors disagree?" The scholarly gentlemen who have devoted special attention to the matter, advance conflicting opinions.

Frederick Locker-Lampson, doubtless the greatest master of the art, both in a critical and creative way, allows wide latitude of discretion. But so infallible is his individual judgment and so unerring his taste, that it is with him, a case of "Know the Rules, and when to break them."

He asserts that "*Vers de Société* by no means need be confined to topics of conventional life."

Contradicting this, is the word of W. Davenport Adams, whose collection of "Songs of Society; from ANNE to VICTORIA," admirably supplements Mr. Locker-Lampson's earlier collection.

Mr. Adams tells us that "*Vers de Société* should be applied to the poetry of fashionable life alone; should be limited to the doings and sayings of the world of fashion, and should deal exclusively with such things as routs and balls, and dinners and receptions."

Our own American collector, Mr. Brander Matthews, inclines to Mr. Locker-Lampson's views, and therefore prefers the term Familiar Verse, as allowing excursions outside of Vanity Fair; while Mr. Edmund Clarence Stedman again narrows the field by declaring in favor of "the more select order of society verse," which he designates "Patrician Rhymes."

Indeed, authorities on the subject of *Vers de Société* seem somewhat in the position of the charming philosopher of *Wonderland* fame:

"'When *I* use a word,' Humpty Dumpty said, in rather a scornful tone, 'it means just what I choose it to mean—neither more nor less.'

"'The question is,' said Alice, 'whether you *can* make words mean so many different things.'

"'The question is,' said Humpty Dumpty, 'Which is to be the master—that's all.'"

But though there is variance of opinion concerning the limits of the field, there is harmony of conviction regarding the intrinsic qualities of *Vers de Société*.

Mr. Locker-Lampson directs us that it should be "short, graceful, refined, and fanciful, not seldom distinguished by chastened sentiment, and often playful. The tone should not be pitched high; it should be terse and idiomatic, and rather in the conversational key; the rhythm should be crisp and sparkling, and the rhyme frequent and never forced. The entire poem should be marked by tasteful moderation, high finish and completeness; for subordination to the rules of composition, and perfection of execution are of the utmost importance.

"The qualities of brevity and buoyancy are absolutely essential. The poem may be tinctured with a well-bred philosophy, it may be whimsically sad, it may be gay and gallant, it may be playfully malicious or tenderly ironical, it may display lively banter, and it may be satirically facetious; it may even, considering it merely as a work of art, be pagan in its philosophy or trifling in its tone, but it must never be flat, or ponderous, or commonplace."

The remarks of Mr. W. Davenport Adams are much in the same line. He says, "There should be little or no enthusiasm: the Muse should not be over-earnest, nor need it by any means be over-flippant. It is essential to 'Society verse' that it should have the tincture of good-breeding;—that if it is lively, it should be so without being vulgar; and that if it is tender it should be so without being maudlin. Its great distinction should be ease—the entire absence of apparent effort—the presence of that playful spontaneity which proclaims the master."

Professor Brander Matthews, in his able essay on the subject, agrees in general to all these stipulations, and observes: "No doubt, Social verse should have polish, and finish, and the well-bred ease of the man of the world; but it ought also to carry, at least a suggestion of the more serious aspects of life. It should not be frothily frivolous or coldly cynical, any more than it should be broadly comic or boisterously funny. It is at liberty to hint at hidden tears, even when it seems to be wreathed in smiles. It has no right to parade mere cleverness; and it must shun all affectation as it must avoid all self-consciousness. It should appear to possess a colloquial carelessness which is ever shrinking from the commonplace and which has succeeded in concealing every trace of that labor of the literary artist by which alone it has attained their seemingly spontaneous perfection.... It must eschew not merely coarseness or vulgarity, but even free and hearty laughter; and it must refrain from dealing not only with the soul-plumbing abysses of the tragic, but even with the ground-swell of any sweeping emotion. It must keep on the crest of the wave, mid-way between the utter triviality of the murmuring shadows and the silent profundity of the depths that are dumb."

Mr. Edmund Clarence Stedman's views coincide with those above quoted, and are thus briefly summed up: "In fine, the true kind is marked by humor, by spontaneity, joined with extreme elegance of finish, by the quality we call breeding,—above all, by lightness of touch."

These same authorities agree that not every poet may write *Vers de Société*. To quote Mr. Locker-Lampson: "The writer of Occasional verse, in order to be genuinely successful, must not only be something of a poet, but he must also be a man of the world, in the liberal sense of the expression; he must have associated throughout his life with the refined and cultivated members of his species, not merely as an idle bystander, but as a busy actor in the throng."

Mr. Adams corroborates this by saying: "Although a clever literary artist may so far throw himself into the position of a man of society as to be able to write very agreeable Society verse, yet few can hope to write the best and most genuine *Vers de Société* who are not, or have not at one time been, in some measure at any rate, inhabitants of 'Society.'"

As an instance, however, of the disagreement among the doctors, the following may be noted:

Mortimer Collins, himself a writer of *Vers de Société*, declared that the lines by Ben Jonson, beginning,

> "Follow a shadow, it still flies you;"

is the most perfect bit of society verse written in our language. And speaking of the same poem, Mr. W. Davenport Adams says, "I cannot bring myself to look upon Ben Jonson as a 'society poet,' or upon the verses in question as a 'society poem' in the proper sense of the term—in the sense at least, in which I understand them."

So we see, that in a degree, at least, *Vers de Société* is, like Beauty, in the eye of the beholder.

But a consensus of opinion seems to prove that the keynote of *Vers de Société* is lightness, both of theme and treatment. Yet though light, it must not be trashy. It is the lightness of beaten gold-leaf, not the lightness of chaff. It is valuable, not worthless.

The spirit of the work depends on an instant perception and a fine appreciation of values, seen through the medium of a whimsical kindliness.

Let this be expressed with perfect taste and skill, and with a courtly sense of humor, and the result may be classed among those immortal ephemeræ which we call *Vers de Société*.

TO CELIA

DRINK to me only with thine eyes,
And I will pledge with mine;
Or leave a kiss but in the cup,
And I'll not ask for wine.

The thirst, that from the soul doth rise,
Doth ask a drink divine;
But might I of Jove's nectar sip,
I would not change for thine.

I sent thee, late, a rosy wreath,
Not so much honoring thee,
As giving it a hope that there
It could not withered be.

But thou thereon didst only breathe
And sent'st it back to me;
Since when it grows, and smells, I swear,
Not of itself, but thee.

Ben Jonson.

CUPID

BEAUTIES, have you seen this toy,
Called love, a little boy,
Almost naked, wanton, blind,
Cruel now, and then as kind?
If he be amongst ye, say!
He is Venus' runaway.

He hath of marks about him plenty;
Ye shall know him among twenty;
All his body is a fire,
And his breath a flame entire,
That, being shot like lightning in,
Wounds the heart, but not the skin.

He doth bear a golden bow,
And a quiver, hanging low,
Full of arrows, that outbrave
Dian's shafts, where, if he have
Any head more sharp than other,
With that first he strikes his mother.

Trust him not: his words, though sweet,
Seldom with his heart do meet;
All his practice is deceit,
Every gift is but a bait;
Not a kiss but poison bears,
And most treason in his tears.

If by these ye please to know him,
Beauties, be not nice, but show him,

Though ye had a will to hide him.
Now, we hope, ye'll not abide him,
Since ye hear his falser play,
And that he's Venus' runaway.

Ben Jonson.

ROSALIND'S MADRIGAL

LOVE in my bosom like a bee
Doth suck his sweet:
Now with his wings he plays with me,
Now with his feet.
Within mine eyes he makes his nest,
His bed amidst my tender breast:
My kisses are his daily feast,
And yet he robs me of my rest.
Ah, wanton, will ye?

And if I sleep, then percheth he
With pretty flight,
And makes his pillow of my knee
The live-long night.
Strike I my lute, he tunes the string,
He music plays if so I sing,
He lends me every lovely thing:
Yet cruel he my heart doth sting:
Whist, wanton, still ye!

Else I with roses every day
Will whip you hence:
And bind you, when you long to play,
For your offence.
I'll shut mine eyes to keep you in,
I'll make you fast it for your sin,
I'll count your power not worth a pin;
Alas, what hereby shall I win,
If he gainsay me?

What if I beat the wanton boy
With many a rod?
He will repay me with annoy,
Because a god.
Then sit thou safely on my knee,
And let thy bower my bosom be;
Lurk in my eyes I like of thee:
O, Cupid so thou pity me,
Spare not, but play thee.

Thomas Lodge.

ALL THINGS EXCEPT MYSELF I KNOW

I KNOW when milk does flies contain;
I know men by their bravery;
I know fair days from storm and rain;
And what fruit apple-trees supply;
And from their gums the trees descry;
I know when all things smoothly flow;
I know who toil or idle lie;
All things except myself I know.

I know the doublet by the grain;
The monk beneath the hood can spy;
Master from man can ascertain;
I know the nun's veiled modesty;
I know when sportsmen fables ply;
Know fools who scream and dainties stow;
Wine from the butt I certify;
All things except myself I know.

Know horse from mule by tail and mane;
I know their worth or high or low;
Bell, Beatrice, I know the twain;
I know each chance of cards and die;
I know what visions prophesy,
Bohemian heresies, I trow;
I know men of each quality;
All things except myself I know.

ENVOY

Prince, I know all things 'neath the sky,

Pale cheeks from those of rosy glow;
I know death whence can no man fly;
All things except myself I know.

François Villon.

CUPID AND CAMPASPE

CUPID and my Campaspe played
At cards for kisses; Cupid paid.
He stakes his quiver, bow, and arrows,
His mother's doves and team of sparrows;
Loses them too; then down he throws
The coral of his lip, the rose
Growing on his cheek, but none knows how;
With these the crystal of his brow,
And then the dimple of his chin:—
All these did my Campaspe win.
At last he set her both his eyes;
She won, and Cupid blind did rise.
O Love! has she done this to thee?
What shall, alas, become of me!

John Lilly.

A DITTY

MY true love hath my heart, and I have his,
By just exchange one to the other given:
I hold his dear, and mine he cannot miss,
There never was a better bargain driven:
My true love hath my heart, and I have his.

His heart in me keeps him and me in one,
My heart in him his thoughts and senses guides:
He loves my heart, for once it was his own,
I cherish his because in me it bides:
My true love hath my heart, and I have his.

Sir Philip Sidney.

SONG FROM "TWELFTH NIGHT"

O MISTRESS mine! where are you roaming?
O! stay and hear; your true love's coming,
That can sing both high and low:
Trip no further, pretty sweeting;
Journeys end in lovers' meeting,
Every wise man's son doth know.

What is love? 'tis not hereafter:
Present mirth hath present laughter;
What's to come is still unsure:
In delay there lies no plenty;
Then come kiss me, sweet and twenty,
Youth's a stuff will not endure.

William Shakespeare.

SIGH NO MORE
(From "*Much Ado About Nothing*")

SIGH no more, ladies, sigh no more,

Men were deceivers ever;

One foot in sea, and one on shore,

To one thing constant never;

Then sigh not so,

But let them go,

And be you blithe and bonny;

Converting all your sounds of woe

Into hey nonny, nonny.

Sing no more ditties, sing no more,

Of dumps so dull and heavy;

The fraud of men was ever so,

Since summer first was leavy:

Then sigh not so,

But let them go,

And be you blithe and bonny;

Converting all your sounds of woe

Into hey nonny, nonny.

William Shakespeare.

PHILLIDA AND CORYDON

IN the merry month of May,
In a morn by break of day,
With a troop of damsels playing
Forth I rode, forsooth, a-maying,
When anon by a woodside,
Where as May was in his pride,
I espied, all alone,
Phillida and Corydon.

Much ado there was, God wot!
He would love, and she would not:
She said, never man was true:
He says, none was false to you.
He said, he had loved her long:
She says, Love should have no wrong.

Corydon would kiss her then,
She says, maids must kiss no men,
Till they do for good and all.
Then she made the shepherd call
All the heavens to witness, truth
Never loved a truer youth.

Thus, with many a pretty oath,
Yea, and nay, and faith and troth!—
Such as silly shepherds use
When they will not love abuse;
Love, which had been long deluded,
Was with kisses sweet concluded:
And Phillida, with garlands gay,

Was made the lady of the May.

Nicholas Breton.

CHERRY-RIPE

THERE is a garden in her face
Where roses and white lilies blow;
A heavenly paradise is that place,
Wherein all pleasant fruits do grow;
There cherries grow that none may buy,
Till cherry-ripe themselves do cry.

Those cherries fairly do enclose
Of Orient pearl a double row,
Which when her lovely laughter shows,
They look like rose-buds fill'd with snow;
Yet them no peer or prince may buy,
Till cherry-ripe themselves do cry.

Her eyes like angels watch them still;
Her brows like bended bows do stand,
Threat'ning with piercing frowns to kill
All that approach with eye or hand
These sacred cherries to come nigh,—
Till cherry-ripe themselves do cry!

Richard Allison.

SEND BACK MY LONG-STRAY'D EYES TO ME

SEND back my long-stray'd eyes to me,
Which, O! too long have dwelt on thee:
But if from you they've learnt such ill,
To sweetly smile,
And then beguile,
Keep the deceivers, keep them still.

Send home my harmless heart again,
Which no unworthy thought could stain;
But if it has been taught by thine
To forfeit both
Its word and oath,
Keep it, for then 'tis none of mine.

Yet send me back my heart and eyes,
For I'll know all thy falsities;
That I one day may laugh, when thou
Shalt grieve and mourn—
Of one the scorn,
Who proves as false as thou art now.

John Donne.

PACK CLOUDS AWAY

PACK clouds away, and welcome day,
With night we banish sorrow:
Sweet air, blow soft, mount, lark, aloft,
To give my love good-morrow.
Wings from the wind to please her mind,
Notes from the lark I'll borrow;
Bird, prune thy wing! nightingale sing!
To give my love good-morrow,
To give my love good-morrow,
Notes from them all I'll borrow.

Wake from thy nest, robin-redbreast!
Sing, birds, in every furrow,
And from each bill let music shrill
Give my fair love good-morrow!
Blackbird and thrush, in every bush,
Stare, linnet, and cock-sparrow,
You pretty elves, amongst yourselves,
Sing my fair love good-morrow.
To give my love good-morrow,
Sing, birds, in every furrow.

Thomas Heywood.

SHALL I, WASTING IN DESPAIR

SHALL I, wasting in despair,
Die because a woman's fair?
Or make pale my cheek with care,
'Cause another's rosy are?
Be she fairer than the day,
Or the flowery meads in May,
If she be not so to me,
What care I how fair she be!

Should my foolish heart be pined
'Cause I see a woman kind?
Or a well disposèd nature
Joinèd with a lovely feature?
Be she meeker, kinder, than
Turtle-dove or pelican,
If she be not so to me,
What care I how kind she be!

Shall a woman's virtues move
Me to perish for her love?
Or, her merit's value known,
Make me quite forget my own?
Be sure with that goodness blest
Which may gain her name of best,
If she seem not such to me,
What care I how good she be!

'Cause her fortune seems too high,
Shall I play the fool and die?
Those that bear a noble mind,

Where they want of richness find,
Think what with them they would do
Who, without them, dare to woo—
And, unless that mind I see,
What care I how great she be!

Great, or good, or kind, or fair,
I will ne'er the more despair:
If she love me, this believe,
I will die ere she shall grieve:
If she slight me when I woo,
I can scorn and let her go:
For, if she be not for me,
What care I for whom she be!

George Wither.

TO THE VIRGINS TO MAKE MUCH OF TIME

GATHER ye rose-buds while ye may,
Old Time is still a-flying;
And this same flower that smiles to-day,
To-morrow will be dying.

The glorious lamp of heaven, the Sun,
The higher he's a getting,
The sooner will his race be run,
And nearer he's to setting.

That age is best, which is the first,
When youth and blood are warmer;
But being spent, the worse, and worst
Times still succeed the former.

Then be not coy, but use your time,
And while you may, go marry:
For having lost but once your prime,
You may forever tarry.

Robert Herrick.

THE BRACELET

WHEN I tie about thy wrist,
Julia, this my silken twist,
For what other reason is't

But to show thee how, in part,
Thou my pretty captive art?
—But thy bond-slave is my heart.

'Tis but silk that bindeth thee,
Snap the thread, and thou art free;
But 'tis otherwise with me:

I am bound, and fast bound, so
That from thee I cannot go:
If I could I would not so!

Robert Herrick.

AN OLD RHYME

I DARE not ask a kisse,
I dare not beg a smile,
Lest having that or this,
I might grow proud the while.
No, no, the utmost share
Of my desire shall be
Only to kisse the aire
That lately kissed thee.

Anonymous.

LOVE ME NOT FOR COMELY GRACE

LOVE me not for comely grace,
For my pleasing eye or face,
Nor for any outward part,
No, nor for my constant heart;
For those may fail or turn to ill,
So thou and I shall sever:
Keep therefore a true woman's eye,
And love me still, but know not why.
So hast thou the same reason still
To dote upon me ever.

Anonymous.

ON A GIRDLE

THAT which her slender waist confined,
Shall now my joyful temples bind;
No monarch but would give his crown
His arms might do what this has done.

It was my Heaven's extremest sphere,
The pale which held that lovely dear.
My joy, my grief, my hope, my love
Did all within this circle move!

A narrow compass! and yet there
Dwelt all that's good, and all that's fair;
Give me but what this riband bound,
Take all the rest the sun goes round.

Edmund Waller.

TO MY LOVE

I PR'YTHEE send me back my heart,
Since I can not have thine;
For if from yours you will not part,
Why then should'st thou have mine?

Yet now I think on't, let it lie;
To find it, were in vain:
For thou'st a thief in either eye
Would steal it back again.

Why should two hearts in one breast lie,
And yet not lodge together?
O love! where is thy sympathy,
If thus our breasts you sever?

But love is such a mystery
I can not find it out;
For when I think I'm best resolved,
I then am in most doubt.

Then farewell care, and farewell woe,
I will no longer pine;
For I'll believe I have her heart,
As much as she has mine.

Sir John Suckling.

TO ALTHEA (FROM PRISON)

WHEN Love with unconfined wings
Hovers within my gates,
And my divine Althea brings
To whisper at the grates;
When I lie tangled in her hair,
And fettered to her eye,
The birds that wanton in the air
Know no such liberty.

When flowing cups run swiftly round
With no allaying Thames,
Our careless heads with roses bound,
Our hearts with loyal flames;
When thirsty grief in wine we steep,
When healths and draughts go free,
Fishes that tipple in the deep
Know no such liberty.

When, like committed linnets, I
With shriller throat shall sing
The sweetness, mercy, majesty,
And glories of my King;
When I shall voice aloud how good
He is, how great should be,
Enlargèd winds that curl the flood
Know no such liberty.

Stone walls do not a prison make,
Nor iron bars a cage;
Minds innocent and quiet take

That for an hermitage:
If I have freedom in my love,
And in my soul am free,
Angels alone that soar above
Enjoy such liberty.

Richard Lovelace.

SONG

HEARS not my Phyllis how the birds
Their feathered mates salute?
They tell their passion in their words;
Must I alone be mute?
Phyllis, without frown or smile,
Sat and knotted all the while.

The god of love in thy bright eyes
Does like a tyrant reign;
But in thy heart a child he lies,
Without his dart or flame.
Phyllis without frown or smile,
Sat and knotted all the while.

So many months in silence past,
And yet in raging love,
Might well deserve one word at last
My passion should approve.
Phyllis, without frown or smile,
Sat and knotted all the while.

Must then your faithful swain expire,
And not one look obtain,
Which he, to soothe his fond desire,
Might pleasantly explain?
Phyllis, without frown or smile,
Sat and knotted all the while.

Sir Charles Sedley.

THE DESPAIRING LOVER

DISTRACTED with care,
For Phyllis the fair,
Since nothing can move her,
Poor Damon, her lover,
Resolves in despair
No longer to languish,
Nor bear so much anguish;
But, mad with his love,
To a precipice goes,
Where a leap from above
Will soon finish his woes.

When, in rage, he came there,
Beholding how steep
The sides did appear,
And the bottom how deep;
His torments projecting,
And sadly reflecting
That a lover forsaken
A new lover may get;
But a neck, when once broken,
Can never be set:

And that he could die
Whenever he would;
But that he could live
But as long as he could;
How grievous soever
The torment might grow,

He scorned to endeavour
To finish it so.
But hold, unconcern'd,
At the thoughts of the pain,
He calmly return'd
To his cottage again.

William Walsh.

CUPID MISTAKEN

AS after noon, one summer's day,
Venus stood bathing in a river;
Cupid a-shooting went that way,
New strung his bow, new fill'd his quiver.

With skill he chose his sharpest dart:
With all his might his bow he drew:
Swift to his beauteous parent's heart
The too-well-guided arrow flew.

"I faint! I die!" the goddess cried:
"O cruel, could'st thou find none other
To wreak thy spleen on: Parricide!
Like Nero, thou hast slain thy mother."

Poor Cupid, sobbing, scarce could speak;
"Indeed, mama, I did not know ye:
Alas! how easy my mistake?
I took you for your likeness, Chloe."

Matthew Prior.

THE CONTRAST

IN London I never know what I'd be at,

Enraptured with this, and enchanted with that;

I'm wild with the sweets of variety's plan,

And Life seems a blessing too happy for man.

But the Country, Lord help me! sets all matters right;

So calm and composing from morning to night;

Oh! it settles the spirits when nothing is seen

But an ass on a common, a goose on a green.

In town if it rain, why it damps not our hope,

The eye has her choice, and the fancy her scope

What harm though it pour whole nights or whole days?

It spoils not our prospects, or stops not our ways.

In the country what bliss, when it rains in the fields,

To live on the transports that shuttlecock yields;

Or go crawling from window to window, to see

A pig on a dung-hill, or crow on a tree.

In London if folks ill together are put,

A bow may be dropt, and a quiz may be cut;

We change without end; and if lazy or ill,

All wants are at hand, and all wishes at will.

In the country you're nail'd, like a pale in the park,

To some stick of a neighbour that's cramm'd in the ark;

And 'tis odds, if you're hurt, or in fits tumble down,

You reach death ere the doctor can reach you from town.

In London how easy we visit and meet,

Gay pleasure's the theme, and sweet smiles are our treat;

Our morning's a round of good-humoured delight,
And we rattle, in comfort, to pleasure at night.

In the country, how sprightly! our visits we make
Through ten miles of mud, for Formality's sake;
With the coachman in drink, and the moon in a fog,
And no thought in our head but a ditch or a bog.

In London the spirits are cheerful and light,
All places are gay and all faces are bright;
We've ever new joys, and revived by each whim,
Each day on a fresh tide of pleasure we swim.

But how gay in the country! what summer delight
To be waiting for winter from morning to night!
Then the fret of impatience gives exquisite glee
To relish the sweet rural subjects we see.

In town we've no use for the skies overhead,
For when the sun rises then we go to bed;
And as to that old-fashion'd virgin the moon;
She shines out of season, like satin in June.

In the country these planets delightfully glare
Just to show us the object we want isn't there;
O, how cheering and gay, when their beauties arise,
To sit and gaze round with the tears in one's eyes!

But 'tis in the country alone we can find
That happy resource, that relief of the mind,
When, drove to despair, our last efforts we make,
And drag the old fish-pond, for novelty's sake:

Indeed, I must own, tis a pleasure complete

To see ladies well draggled and wet in their feet;
But what is all that to the transport we feel
When we capture, in triumph, two toads and an eel?

I have heard tho', that love in a cottage is sweet,
When two hearts in one link of soft sympathy meet:
That's to come—for as yet I, alas! am a swain
Who require, I own it, more links to my chain.

Your magpies and stock-doves may flirt among trees,
And chatter their transports in groves, if they please:
But a house is much more to my taste than a tree,
And for groves, O! a good grove of chimneys for me.

In the country, if Cupid should find a man out,
The poor tortured victim mopes hopeless about;
But in London, thank Heaven! our peace is secure,
Where for one eye to kill, there's a thousand to cure.

I know love's a devil, too subtle to spy,
That shoots through the soul, from the beam of an eye;
But in London these devils so quick fly about,
That a new devil still drives an old devil out.

In town let me live then, in town let me die,
For in truth I can't relish the country, not I.
If one must have a villa in summer to dwell,
O, give me the sweet shady side of Pall Mall!

Charles Morris.

OH, TELL ME HOW TO WOO THEE

IF doughty deeds my lady please,
Right soon I'll mount my steed;
And strong his arm, and fast his seat,
That bears frae me the meed.
I'll wear thy colors in my cap,
Thy picture in my heart;
And he that bends not to thine eye
Shall rue it to his smart.
Then tell me how to woo thee, love;
Oh, tell me how to woo thee!
For thy dear sake, nae care I'll take,
Though ne'er another trow me.

If gay attire delight thine eye,
I'll dight me in array;
I'll tend thy chamber door all night,
And squire thee all the day.
If sweetest sounds can win thine ear,
These sounds I'll strive to catch;
Thy voice I'll steal to woo thysel'—
That voice that none can match.
Then tell me how to woo thee, love, etc.

But if fond love thy heart can gain,
I never broke a vow;
Nae maiden lays her skaith to me;
I never loved but you.
For you alone I ride the ring,
For you I wear the blue;

For you alone I strive to sing—
Oh, tell me how to woo!
Then tell me how to woo thee, love, etc.

Robert Graham.

SONG FROM "THE DUENNA"

I NE'ER could any lustre see
In eyes that would not look on me;
I ne'er saw nectar on a lip,
But where my own did hope to sip.
Has the maid who seeks my heart
Cheeks of rose, untouched by art?
I will own thy color true,
When yielding blushes aid their hue.
Is her hand so soft and pure?
I must press it, to be sure;
Nor can I be certain then,
Till it, grateful, press again.
Must I, with attentive eye,
Watch her heaving bosom sigh?
I will do so when I see
That heaving bosom sigh for me.

Richard Brinsley Sheridan.

THE RACES
A BALLAD

O GEORGE! I've been, I'll tell you where,
But first prepare yourself for raptures;
To paint this charming heavenly fair,
And paint her well, would ask whole chapters.

Fine creatures I've viewed many a one,
With lovely shapes and angel faces,
But I have seen them all outdone
By this sweet maid, at —— Races.

Lords, Commoners, alike she rules,
Takes all who view her by surprise,
Makes e'en the wisest look like fools,
Nay more, makes fox-hunters look wise.

Her shape—'tis elegance and ease,
Unspoiled by art or modern dress,
But gently tapering by degrees,
And finely, "beautifully less."

Her foot—it was so wondrous small,
So thin, so round, so slim, so neat,
The buckle fairly hid it all,
And seemed to sink it with the weight.

And just above the spangled shoe,
Where many an eye did often glance,
Sweetly retiring from the view,
And seen by stealth, and seen by chance;

Two slender ankles peeping out,

Stood like Love's heralds, to declare,
That all within the petticoat
Was firm and full, and "round, and fair."

And then she dances—better far
Than heart can think, or tongue can tell,
Not Heinel, Banti, or Guimar,
E'er moved so graceful and so well.

So easy glide her beauteous limbs,
True as the echo to the sound,
She seems, as through the dance she skims,
To tread on air, and scorn the ground.

And there is lightning in her eye,
One glance alone might well inspire
The clay-cold breast of Apathy,
Or bid the frozen heart catch fire.

And zephyr on her lovely lips
Has spread his choicest, sweetest roses,
And there his heavenly nectar sips,
And there in breathing sweet reposes.

And there's such music when she speaks,
You may believe me when I tell ye,
I'd rather hear her than the squeaks
Or far famed squalls of Gabrielli.

And sparkling wit and steady sense,
In that fair form with beauty vie,
But tinged with virgin diffidence,
And the soft blush of modesty.

Had I the treasures of the world,
All the sun views or the seas borrow
(Else may I to the devil be hurled),
I'd lay them at her feet to-morrow.

But as we Bards reap only Bays,
Nor much of that, though nought grows on it,
I'll beat my brains to sound her praise,
And hammer them into a sonnet.

And if she deign one charming smile
The blest reward of all my labours,
I'll never grudge my pains or toil,
But pity the dull squires, my neighbours.

George Ellis.

TO LADY ANNE HAMILTON

TOO late I stayed, forgive the crime,—
Unheeded flew the hours;
How noiseless falls the foot of Time
That only treads on flowers!

What eye with clear account remarks
The ebbing of his glass,
When all its sands are diamond sparks,
That dazzle as they pass?

Ah! who to sober measurement
Time's happy swiftness brings,
When birds of paradise have lent
Their plumage for his wings?

Hon. William R. Spencer.

TO MRS. LEIGH UPON HER WEDDING-DAY

WHILE all to this auspicious day
Well pleased their heartfelt homage pay
And sweetly smile and softly say
A hundred civic speeches;
My Muse shall strike her tuneful strings,
Nor scorn the gift her duty brings,
Tho' humble be the theme she sings,—
A pair of shooting breeches.

Soon shall the tailor's subtle art
Have made them tight, and spruce, and smart,
And fastened well in every part
With twenty thousand stitches;
Mark then the moral of my song,
Oh, may your lives but prove as strong,
And wear as well, and last as long,
As these, my shooting breeches.

And when, to ease the load of life,
Of private care, and public strife,
My lot shall give to me a wife,
I ask not rank or riches;
For worth like thine alone I pray,
Temper like thine serene and gay,
And formed like thee to give away,
Not wear herself, the breeches.

George Canning.

NAMES

I ASKED my fair, one happy day,
What I should call her in my lay;
By what sweet name from Rome or Greece
Lalage, Neæra, Chloris,
Sappho, Lesbia, or Doris,
Arethusa or Lucrece.

"Ah!" replied my gentle fair,
"Beloved, what are names but air?
Choose you whatever suits the line;
Call me Daphne, call me Chloris,
Call me Lalage or Doris,
Only, only call me thine."

Samuel T. Coleridge.

THE EXCHANGE

WE pledged our hearts, my love and I,—
I in my arms the maiden clasping:
I could not tell the reason why,
But oh! I trembled like an aspen.

Her father's love she bade me gain;
I went, and shook like any reed!
I strove to act the man in vain!
We had exchanged our hearts indeed.

Samuel T. Coleridge.

DEFIANCE

CATCH her and hold her if you can . . .
Shuts, opens, and then holds it spread
In threatening guise above your head.
Ah! why did you not start before
She reached the porch and closed the door?
Simpleton! will you never learn
That girls and time will not return;
Of each you should have made the most;
Once gone, they are forever lost.
In vain your knuckles knock your brow,
In vain will you remember how
Like a slim brook the gamesome maid
Sparkled, and ran into the shade.

Walter Savage Landor.

HER LIPS

OFTEN I have heard it said
That her lips are ruby-red.
Little heed I what they say,
I have seen as red as they.
Ere she smiled on other men,
Real rubies were they then.

When she kiss'd me once in play,
Rubies were less bright than they,
And less bright were those that shone
In the palace of the Sun.
Will they be as bright again?
Not if kiss'd by other men.

Walter Savage Landor.

COMMINATION

TAKING my walk the other day,
I saw a little girl at play,
So pretty, 'twould not be amiss,
Thought I, to venture on a kiss.
Fiercely the little girl began—
"I wonder at you, nasty man!"
And all four fingers were applied,
And crimson pinafore beside,
To wipe what venom might remain,—
"Do if you dare the like again;
I have a mind to teach you better,"
And I too had a mind to let her.

Walter Savage Landor.

MARGARET AND DORA

MARGARET'S beauteous—Grecian arts
Ne'er drew form completer,
Yet why, in my heart of hearts,
Hold I Dora's sweeter?

Dora's eyes of heavenly blue
Pass all paintings' reach,
Ringdove's notes are discord to
The music of her speech.

Artists Margaret's smile receive,
And on canvas show it;
But for perfect worship leave
Dora to her poet.

Thomas Campbell.

A CERTAIN YOUNG LADY

THERE'S a certain young lady,
Who's just in her heyday,
And full of all mischief, I ween;
So teasing! so pleasing!
Capricious! delicious!
And you know very well whom I mean.

With an eye dark as night,
Yet than noonday more bright,
Was ever a black eye so keen?
It can thrill with a glance,
With a beam can entrance,
And you know very well whom I mean.

With a stately step—such as
You'd expect in a duchess—
And a brow might distinguish a queen,
With a mighty proud air,
That says "touch me who dare,"
And you know very well whom I mean.

With a toss of the head
That strikes one quite dead,
But a smile to revive one again;
That toss so appalling!
That smile so enthralling!
And you know very well whom I mean.

Confound her! devil take her!—
A cruel heart-breaker—

But hold! see that smile so serene.
God love her! God bless her!
May nothing distress her!
You know very well whom I mean.

Heaven help the adorer
Who happens to bore her,
The lover who wakens her spleen;
But too blest for a sinner
Is he who shall win her,
And you know very well whom I mean.

Washington Irving.

SONG

WHO has robbed the ocean cave,
To tinge thy lips with coral hue?
Who from India's distant wave
For thee those pearly treasures drew?
Who from yonder orient sky
Stole the morning of thine eye?

Thousand charms, thy form to deck,
From sea, and earth, and air are torn;
Roses bloom upon thy cheek,
On thy breath their fragrance borne.
Guard thy bosom from the day,
Lest thy snows should melt away.

But one charm remains behind,
Which mute earth can ne'er impart;
Nor in ocean wilt thou find,
Nor in the circling air, a heart.
Fairest! wouldst thou perfect be,
Take, oh, take that heart from me.

John Shaw.

THE TIME I'VE LOST IN WOOING

THE time I've lost in wooing,
In watching and pursuing
The light that lies
In woman's eyes,
Has been my heart's undoing.
Tho' wisdom oft has sought me,
I scorn'd the lore she brought me,
My only books
Were woman's looks,
And folly's all they taught me.

Her smile when Beauty granted,
I hung with gaze enchanted,
Like him the sprite
Whom maids by night
Oft meet in glen that's haunted.
Like him, too, Beauty won me;
But when the spell was on me,
If once their ray
Was turn'd away,
O! winds could not outrun me.

And are those follies going?
And is my proud heart growing
Too cold or wise
For brilliant eyes
Again to set it glowing?
No—vain, alas! th' endeavor
From bonds so sweet to sever;—

Poor Wisdom's chance
Against a glance
Is now as weak as ever.

Thomas Moore.

WHEN I LOVED YOU

WHEN I loved you, I can't but allow
I had many an exquisite minute;
But the scorn that I feel for you now
Hath even more luxury in it!

Thus, whether we're on or we're off,
Some witchery seems to await you;
To love you is pleasant enough,
And oh! 'tis delicious to hate you!

Thomas Moore.

REASON, FOLLY, AND BEAUTY

REASON, and Folly, and Beauty, they say
Went on a party of pleasure one day:
Folly play'd
Around the maid,
The bells of his cap rang merrily out;
While Reason took
To his sermon-book—
O! which was the pleasanter no one need doubt,
Which was the pleasanter no one need doubt.

Beauty, who likes to be thought very sage,
Turn'd for a moment to Reason's dull page,
Till Folly said,
"Look here, sweet maid!"—
The sight of his cap brought her back to herself,
While Reason read
His leaves of lead,
With no one to mind him, poor sensible elf!
No,—no one to mind him, poor sensible elf!

Then Reason grew jealous of Folly's gay cap;
Had he that on, he her heart might entrap—
"There it is,"
Quoth Folly, "old quiz!"
(Folly was always good-natured, 'tis said.)
"Under the sun
There's no such fun,
As Reason with my cap and bells on his head,
Reason with my cap and bells on his head!"

But Reason the head-dress so awkwardly wore,
That Beauty now liked him still less than before:
While Folly took
Old Reason's book,
And twisted the leaves in a cap of such *ton*,
That Beauty vow'd
(Tho' not aloud)
She liked him still better in that than his own,
Yes,—liked him still better in that than his own.

Thomas Moore.

TIRESOME SPRING!

I HAVE watched her at the window
Through long days of snow and wind,
Till I learnt to love the shadow
That would flit across her blind.
'Twixt the lime-tree's leafless branches
In the dusk my eyes I'd strain:
Now the boughs are thick with foliage,—
Tiresome Spring! you've come again!

Now, behind that screen of verdure
Is my angel lost to view;
And no longer for the robins
Will her white hands bread-crumbs strew.
Never in the frosts of winter,
Did those robins beg in vain;
Now, alas! the snow has melted,—
Tiresome Spring! you've come again!

'Tis kind winter that I wish for;—
How I long to hear the hail
Rattling on deserted pavements,
Dancing in the stormy gale!
For I then could see her windows,
Watch my darling through each pane
Now the lime-trees are in blossom,—
Tiresome Spring! you've come again!

Béranger.

ROSETTE

YES! I know you're very fair;
And the rose-bloom of your cheek,
And the gold-crown of your hair,
Seem of tender love to speak.
But to me they speak in vain,
I am growing old, my pet—
Ah, if I could love you now
As I used to love Rosette!

In your carriage every day
I can see you bow and smile;
Lovers your least word obey,
Mistress you of every wile.
She was poor, and went on foot,
Badly drest, you know,—and yet,—
Ah! if I could love you now
As I used to love Rosette!

You are clever, and well known
For your wit so quick and free;—
Now, Rosette, I blush to own,
Scarcely knew her A B C;
But she had a potent charm
In my youth:—ah, vain regret!
If I could but love you now
As I used to love Rosette!

Béranger.

SHE IS SO PRETTY

SHE is so pretty, the girl I love,
Her eyes are tender and deep and blue
As the summer night in the skies above,
As violets seen through a mist of dew.
How can I hope, then, her heart to gain?
She is so pretty, and I am so plain!

She is so pretty, so fair to see!
Scarcely she's counted her nineteenth spring,
Fresh, and blooming, and young,—ah me!
Why do I thus her praises sing?
Surely from me 'tis a senseless strain,
She is so pretty, and I am so plain!

She is so pretty, so sweet and dear,
There's many a lover who loves her well;
I may not hope, I can only fear,
Yet shall I venture my love to tell? . . .
Ah! I have pleaded, and not in vain—
Though she's so pretty, and I am so plain.

Béranger.

RONDEAU

JENNY kissed me when we met,
Jumping from the chair she sat in;
Time, you thief, who love to get
Sweets into your list, put that in:
Say I'm weary, say I'm sad,
Say that health and wealth have missed me,
Say I'm growing old, but add,
Jenny kissed me!

Leigh Hunt.

STOLEN FRUIT

WE the fairies, blithe and antic,
Of dimensions not gigantic,
Though the moonshine mostly keep us,
Oft in orchards frisk and peep us.

Stolen sweets are always sweeter,
Stolen kisses much completer,
Stolen looks are nice in chapels,
Stolen, stolen be your apples.

When to bed the world is bobbing,
Then's the time for orchard-robbing;
Yet the fruit were scarce worth peeling
Were it not for stealing, stealing.

Leigh Hunt (from the Italian).

LOVE AND AGE

I PLAY'D with you 'mid cowslips blowing
When I was six and you were four:
When garlands weaving, flower balls throwing,
Were pleasures soon to please no more.
Thro' groves and meads, o'er grass and heather,
With little playmates, to and fro,
We wander'd hand in hand together;
But that was sixty years ago.

You grew a lovely roseate maiden,
And still our early love was strong;
Still with no care our days were laden,
They glided joyously along;
And I did love you very dearly—
How dearly, words want power to show;
I thought your heart was touched as nearly;
But that was fifty years ago.

Then other lovers came around you,
Your beauty grew from year to year,
And many a splendid circle found you
The centre of its glittering sphere.
I saw you then, first vows forsaking,
On rank and wealth your hand bestow;
O, then, I thought my heart was breaking,—
But that was forty years ago.

And I lived on to wed another:
No cause she gave me to repine;
And when I heard you were a mother,

I did not wish the children mine.
My own young flock, in fair progression,
Made up a pleasant Christmas row:
My joy in them was past expression;—
But that was thirty years ago.

You grew a matron plump and comely,
You dwelt in fashion's brightest blaze;
My earthly lot was far more homely;
But I too had my festal days.
No merrier eyes have ever glistened
Around the hearth-stone's wintry glow,
Than when my youngest child was christen'd:—
But that was twenty years ago.

Time passed. My eldest girl was married
And I now am a grandsire grey;
One pet of four years old I've carried
Among the wild-flower'd meads to play.
In our old fields of childish pleasure,
Where now, as then, the cowslips blow,
She fills her basket's ample measure,—
And that is not ten years ago.

But tho' first love's impassion'd blindness
Has pass'd away in colder light,
I still have thought of you with kindness,
And shall do, till our last good-night.
The ever rolling silent hours
Will bring a time we shall not know,
When our young days of gathering flowers

Will be an hundred years ago.

Thomas L. Peacock.

CLUBS

IF any man loves comfort and has little cash to buy it, he
Should get into a crowded club—a most select society,—
While solitude and mutton-cutlets serve *infelix uxor*, he
May have his club, like Hercules, and revel there in luxury.

Yes, clubs knock taverns on the head. E'en Hatchett's can't demolish 'em;
Joy grieves to see their magnitude, and Long longs to abolish 'em.
The Inns are out. Hotels for single men scarce keep alive on it,
While none but houses that are in the family way thrive on it.

There's first the Athenæum Club; so wise, there's not a man of it
That has not sense enough for six—in fact, that is the plan of it.
The very waiters answer you with eloquence Socratical,
And always place the knives and forks in order mathematical.

Then opposite the mental club you'll find the regimental one—
A meeting made of men of war, and yet a very gentle one.
If uniform good living please your palate, here's excess of it.
Especially at private dinners, when they make a mess of it.

E'en Isis has a house in town and Cam abandons her city;
The master now hangs out at the United University.
In common room she gave a rout (a novel freak to hit upon),
Where Masters gave the Mistresses of Arts no chairs to sit upon.

The Union Club is quite superb; its best apartment daily is
The lounge of lawyers, doctors, merchants, beaux, *cum multis aliis*.
At half-past six the joint concern for eighteen pence is given you,
Half-pints of port are sent in ketchup-bottles to enliven you.

The Travellers are in Pall Mall, and smoke cigars so cosily,

And dream they climb the highest Alps or rove the plains of Moselai.
The world for them has nothing new, they have explored all parts of it,
And now they are club-footed, and they sit and look at charts of it.

The Orientals, homeward-bound, now seek their club much sallower,
And while they eat green fat they find their own fat growing yellower.
Their soup is made more savoury, till bile to shadows dwindles 'em,
And neither Moore nor Savory with seidlitz draughts rekindles 'em.

Then there are clubs where persons parliamentary preponderate,
And clubs for men upon the turf (I wonder they ar'n't under it);
Clubs where the winning ways of sharper folks pervert the use of clubs,
Where knaves will make subscribers cry, "Egad! this is the deuce of clubs!"

For country squires the only club in London now is Boodle's, sirs,
The Crockford Club for playful men, the Alfred Club for noodles, sirs:
These are the stages which all men propose to play their parts upon,
For Clubs are what the Londoners have clearly set their hearts upon.

Theodore Hook.

TO ANNE

HOW many kisses do I ask?
Now you set me to my task.
First, sweet Anne, will you tell me
How many waves are in the sea?
How many stars are in the sky?
How many lovers you make sigh?
How many sands are on the shore?
I shall want just one kiss more.

William Maxwell.

SONG

DOST thou idly ask to hear
At what gentle seasons
Nymphs relent, when lovers near
Press the tenderest reasons?
Ah, they give their faith too oft
To the careless wooer;
Maidens' hearts are always soft—
Would that men's were truer!

Woo the fair one, when around
Early birds are singing;
When, o'er all the fragrant ground,
Early herbs are springing:
When the brookside, bank, and grove,
All with blossoms laden,
Shine with beauty, breathe of love,—
Woo the timid maiden.

Woo her when, with rosy blush,
Summer eve is sinking;
When, on rills that softly gush,
Stars are softly winking;
When, through boughs that knit the bower,
Moonlight gleams are stealing;
Woo her, till the gentle hour
Wakes a gentler feeling.

Woo her, when autumnal dyes
Tinge the woody mountain;
When the dropping foliage lies

In the weedy fountain;
Let the scene that tells how fast
Youth is passing over,
Warn her, ere her bloom is past,
To secure her lover.

Woo her when the north winds call
At the lattice nightly;
When within the cheerful hall
Blaze the fagots brightly;
While the wintry tempest round
Sweeps the landscape hoary,
Sweeter in her ears shall sound
Love's delightful story.

William Cullen Bryant.

WHAT IS LONDON'S LAST NEW LION?

WHAT is London's last new lion? Pray, inform me if you can;
Is't a woman of Kamschatka or an Otaheite man?
For my *conversazione* you must send me something new,
Don't forget me! Oh I sigh for the *eclat* of a *debut!*

I am sick of all the "minstrels," all the "brothers" this and that,
Who sing sweetly at the parties, while the ladies laugh and chat;
And the man who play'd upon his chin is *passé*, I suppose
So try and find a gentleman who plays upon his nose.

Send half-a-dozen authors, for they help to fill a rout,
I fear I've worn the literary lionesses out!
Send something biographical, I think that fashion spreads,
But do not send a poet, till you find one with two heads.

The town has grown fastidious, we do not care a straw
For the whiskers of a bandit, or the tail of a bashaw!
And travellers are out of date, I mean to cut them soon,
Unless you send me some one who has travelled to the moon.

Oh, if you send a singer, he must sing without a throat!
Oh, if you send a player, he must harp upon one note!
I must have something marvellous, the marvel makes the man;
What is London's last new lion? Pray, inform me if you can.

Thomas Haynes Bayly.

I'D BE A BUTTERFLY

I'D be a Butterfly born in a bower,
Where roses and lilies and violets meet;
Roving for ever from flower to flower,
And kissing all buds that are pretty and sweet!
I'd never languish for wealth, or for power,
I'd never sigh to see slaves at my feet;
I'd be a Butterfly born in a bower,
Kissing all buds that are pretty and sweet.

O could I pilfer the wand of a fairy,
I'd have a pair of those beautiful wings;
Their summer days' ramble is sportive and airy,
They sleep in a rose when the nightingale sings.
Those who have wealth must be watchful and wary;
Power, alas! nought but misery brings!
I'd be a Butterfly, sportive and airy,
Rock'd in a rose when the nightingale sings!

What, though you tell me each gay little rover
Shrinks from the breath of the first autumn day:
Surely 'tis better when summer is over
To die when all fair things are fading away.
Some in life's winter may toil to discover
Means of procuring a weary delay—
I'd be a Butterfly; living, a rover,
Dying when fair things are fading away!

Thomas Haynes Bayly.

"I MUST COME OUT NEXT SPRING"

I MUST come out next Spring, Mamma,
I must come out next Spring;
To keep me with my Governess
Would be a cruel thing:
Whene'er I see my sisters dress'd
In leno and in lace,—
Miss Twig's apartment seems to be
A miserable place.
I must come out next Spring, Mamma,
I must come out next Spring;
To keep me with my Governess
Would be a cruel thing.

I'm very sick of Grosv'nor Square,
The path within the rails;
I'm weary of Telemachus,
And such outlandish tales:
I hate my French, my vile Chambaud;
In tears I've turn'd his leaves;
Oh! let me Frenchify my hair,
And take to Gigot sleeves.
I must come out next Spring, Mamma,
I must come out next Spring;
To keep me with my Governess
Would be a cruel thing.

I know quite well what I should say
To partners at a ball;
I've got a pretty speech or two,

And they would serve for all.
If an Hussar, I'd praise his horse,
And win a smile from him;
And if a Naval man, I'd lisp,
"Pray, Captain, do you swim?"
I must come out next Spring, Mamma,
I must come out next Spring;
To keep me with my Governess
Would be a cruel thing.

Thomas Haynes Bayly.

"WHY DON'T THE MEN PROPOSE?"

WHY don't the men propose, mamma?
Why don't the men propose?
Each seems just coming to the point,
And then away he goes!
It is no fault of yours, mamma,
That everybody knows;
You fête the finest men in town,
Yet, oh, they won't propose!

I'm sure I've done my best, mamma,
To make a proper match;
For coronets and eldest sons
I'm ever on the watch:
I've hopes when some *distingué* beau
A glance upon me throws;
But though he'll dance, and smile, and flirt,
Alas, he won't propose!

I've tried to win by languishing,
And dressing like a blue;
I've bought big books, and talk'd of them,
As if I read them through!
With hair cropp'd like a man, I've felt
The heads of all the beaux;
But Spurzheim could not touch their hearts,
And oh, they won't propose!

I threw aside the books, and thought
That ignorance was bliss;
I felt convinced that men preferr'd

A simple sort of Miss;
And so I lisp'd out naught beyond
Plain "yeses" or plain "noes,"
And wore a sweet unmeaning smile;
Yet, oh, they won't propose!

Last night, at Lady Ramble's rout,
I heard Sir Harry Gale
Exclaim, "Now, I propose again———"
I started, turning pale;
I really thought my time was come,
I blush'd like any rose;
But, oh! I found 'twas only at
Ecarté he'd propose!

And what is to be done, mamma?
Oh, what is to be done?
I really have no time to lose,
For I am thirty-one.
At balls, I am too often left
Where spinsters sit in rows;
Why won't the men propose, mamma?
Why won't the men propose?

Thomas Haynes Bayly.

ASK AND HAVE

"OH, 'tis time I should talk to your mother,
Sweet Mary," says I;
"Oh, don't talk to my mother," says Mary,
Beginning to cry:
"For my mother says men are deceivers,
And never, I know, will consent;
She says girls in a hurry who marry,
At leisure repent."

"Then, suppose I would talk to your father,
Sweet Mary," says I;
"Oh, don't talk to my father," says Mary,
Beginning to cry:
"For my father he loves me so dearly,
He'll never consent I should go—
If you talk to my father," says Mary,
"He'll surely say, 'No.'"

"Then how shall I get you, my jewel?
Sweet Mary," says I;
"If your father and mother's so cruel,
Most surely I'll die!"
"Oh, never say die, dear," says Mary;
"A way now to save you I see;
Since my parents are both so contrary—
You'd better ask me!"

Samuel Lover.

LINES IN A YOUNG LADY'S ALBUM

A PRETTY task, Miss S——, to ask
A Benedictine pen,
That cannot quite at freedom write
Like those of other men.
No lover's plaint my Muse must paint
To fill this page's span,
But be correct and recollect
I'm not a single man.

Pray only think for pen and ink
How hard to get along,
That may not turn on words that burn,
Or Love, the life of song!
Nine Muses, if I chooses, I
May woo all in a clan,
But one Miss S—— I daren't address—
I'm not a single man.

Scribblers unwed, with little head
May eke it out with heart,
And in their lays it often plays
A rare first-fiddle part:
They make a kiss to rhyme with bliss,
But if I so began,
I have my fears about my ears—
I'm not a single man.

Upon your cheek I may not speak,
Nor on your lip be warm,
I must be wise about your eyes,

And formal with your form;
Of all that sort of thing, in short,
On T. H. Bayly's plan,
I must not twine a single line—
I'm not a single man.

A watchman's part compels my heart
To keep you off its beat,
And I might dare as soon to swear
At you as at your feet.
I can't expire in passion's fire,
As other poets can—
My wife (she's by) won't let me die—
I'm not a single man.

Shut out from love, denied a dove,
Forbidden bow and dart,
Without a groan to call my own,
With neither hand nor heart,
To Hymen vowed, and not allowed
To flirt e'en with your fan,
Here end, as just a friend, I must—
I'm not a single man.

Thomas Hood.

THE TIME OF ROSES

IT was not in the winter
Our loving lot was cast;
It was the time of roses,—
We plucked them as we passed.

That churlish season never frowned
On earthly lovers yet:
Oh, no! the world was newly crowned
With flowers when first we met!

'Twas twilight, and I bade you go,
But still you held me fast;
It was the time of roses,—
We plucked them as we passed.

What else could peer thy glowing cheek,
That tears began to stud?
And when I asked the like of Love,
You snatched a damask bud;

And oped it to the dainty core,
Still glowing to the last.
It was the time of roses,—
We plucked them as we passed.

Thomas Hood.

LOVE

O LOVE! What art thou, Love? the ace of hearts,
Trumping Earth's kings and Queens, and all its suits;
A player masquerading many parts
In life's odd carnival;—A boy that shoots,
From ladies' eyes, such mortal woundy darts;
A gardener, pulling heart's-ease up by the roots;
The Puck of Passion—partly false—part real—
A marriageable maiden's "beau-ideal."

O Love, what art thou, Love? a wicked thing,
Making green misses spoil their work at school;
A melancholy man, cross-gartering?
Grave ripe-faced wisdom made an April fool?
A youngster tilting at a wedding-ring?
A sinner, sitting on a cuttie stool?
A Ferdinand de Something in a hovel,
Helping Matilda Rose to make a novel?

O Love! what art thou, Love? one that is bad
With palpitations of the heart—like mine—
A poor bewildered maid, making so sad
A necklace of her garters—fell design!
A poet gone unreasonably mad,
Ending his sonnets with a hempen line?
O Love!—but whither now? forgive me, pray;
I'm not the first that Love hath led astray.

Thomas Hood.

TO HELEN

IF wandering in a wizard's car
Through yon blue ether, I were able
To fashion of a little star
A taper for my Helen's table;—

"What then?" she asks me with a laugh—
Why, then, with all heaven's lustre glowing,
It would not gild her path with half
The light her love o'er mine is throwing.

Winthrop Mackworth Praed.

THE BELLE OF THE BALL-ROOM

YEARS—years ago,—ere yet my dreams
Had been of being wise or witty,—
Ere I had done with writing themes,
Or yawn'd o'er this infernal Chitty;—
Years—years ago,—while all my joy
Was in my fowling-piece and filly,—
In short, while I was yet a boy,
I fell in love with Laura Lilly.

I saw her at the County Ball:
There, where the sounds of flute and fiddle,
Gave signal sweet, in that old hall,
Of hands across and down the middle,
Hers was the subtlest spell by far
Of all that set young hearts romancing,
She was our queen, our rose, our star;
And then she danced—O Heaven, her dancing!

Dark was her hair, her hand was white;
Her voice was exquisitely tender;
Her eyes were full of liquid light;
I never saw a waist so slender!
Her every look, her every smile
Shot right and left a score of arrows;
I thought 'twas Venus from her Isle,
And wonder'd where she'd left her sparrows.

She talk'd,—of politics or prayers,—
Or Southey's prose, or Wordsworth's sonnets,—
Of danglers—or of dancing bears,

Of battles—or the last new bonnets,
By candlelight, at twelve o'clock,
To me it matter'd not a tittle;
If those bright lips had quoted Locke,
I might have thought they murmur'd Little.
Through sunny May, through sultry June,
I loved her with a love eternal;
I spoke her praises to the moon,
I wrote them to the Sunday Journal:
My mother laugh'd; I soon found out
That ancient ladies have no feeling:
My father frown'd; but how should gout
See any happiness in kneeling?

She was the daughter of a Dean,
Rich, fat, and rather apoplectic;
She had one brother, just thirteen,
Whose color was extremely hectic;
Her grandmother for many a year
Had fed the parish with her bounty;
Her second cousin was a peer,
And Lord Lieutenant of the County.

But titles, and the three per cents,
And mortgages, and great relations,
And India bonds, and tithes, and rents,
Oh what are they to love's sensations?
Black eyes, fair forehead, clustering locks—
Such wealth, such honors, Cupid chooses,
He cares as little for the Stocks,
As Baron Rothschild for the Muses.

She sketch'd; the vale, the wood, the beach,
Grew lovelier from her pencil's shading:
She botanized; I envied each
Young blossom in her boudoir fading:
She warbled Handel; it was grand;
She made the Catalani jealous:
She touch'd the organ; I could stand
For hours and hours to blow the bellows.

She kept an album, too, at home,
Well fill'd with all an album's glories;
Paintings of butterflies, and Rome,
Patterns for trimmings, Persian stories;
Soft songs to Julia's cockatoo,
Fierce odes to Famine and to Slaughter,
And autographs of Prince Leboo,
And recipes for elder-water.

And she was flatter'd, worshipp'd, bored;
Her steps were watched, her dress was noted;
Her poodle dog was quite adored,
Her sayings were extremely quoted;
She laugh'd, and every heart was glad,
As if the taxes were abolish'd;
She frown'd, and every look was sad,
As if the Opera were demolish'd.

She smiled on many, just for fun,—
I knew that there was nothing in it;
I was the first—the only one
Her heart had thought of for a minute.—

I knew it, for she told me so,
In phrase which was divinely moulded;
She wrote a charming hand,—and oh!
How sweetly all her notes were folded!

Our love was like most other loves;—
A little glow, a little shiver,
A rose-bud, and a pair of gloves,
And "Fly not yet"—upon the river;
Some jealousy of some one's heir,
Some hopes of dying broken-hearted,
A miniature, a lock of hair,
The usual vows,—and then we parted.

We parted; months and years roll'd by;
We met again four summers after:
Our parting was all sob and sigh;
Our meeting was all mirth and laughter:
For in my heart's most secret cell
There had been many other lodgers;
And she was not the ball-room's Belle,
But only—Mrs. Something Rogers!

Winthrop Mackworth Praed.

AMY'S CRUELTY

FAIR Amy of the terraced House!
Assist me to discover
Why you, who would not hurt a mouse,
Can torture so a lover?

You give your coffee to the cat,
You stroke the dog for coming,
And all your face grows kinder at
The little brown bee's humming.

But when he haunts your door—the town
Marks coming and marks going—
You seem to have stitched your eyelids down
To that long piece of sewing!

You never give a look, not you,
Nor drop him a "Good-morning,"
To keep his long day warm and blue,
So fretted by your scorning.

She shook her head—"The mouse and bee
For crumb or flower will linger;
The dog is happy at my knee,
The cat purrs at my finger.

"But he—to him, the least thing given
Means great things at a distance:
He wants my world, my sun, my heaven,
Soul, body, whole existence.

"They say love gives as well as takes;
But I'm a simple maiden,—

My mother's first smile when she wakes
I still have smiled and prayed in.

"I only know my mother's love,
Which gives all and asks nothing;
And this new loving sets the groove
Too much the way of loathing.

"Unless he gives me all in 'change,
I forfeit all things by him;
The risk is terrible and strange;
I tremble, doubt—deny him.

"His sweetest friend, or hardest foe,
Best angel or worst devil,
I either hate—or love him so,
I can't be merely civil!

"Such love's a cowslip-ball to fling,
A moment's pretty pastime;
I give—all me, if anything,
The first time, and the last time.

"Dear neighbour of the trellised house!
A man should murmur never,
Though treated worse than dog or mouse,
Till doted on for ever."

Elizabeth Barrett Browning.

BEWARE!

I KNOW a maiden fair to see,
Take care!
She can both false and friendly be,
Beware! Beware!
Trust her not,
She is fooling thee!

She has two eyes, so soft and brown,
Take care!
She gives a side-glance and looks down,
Beware! Beware!
Trust her not,
She is fooling thee!

And she has hair of a golden hue,
Take care!
And what she says, it is not true,
Beware! Beware!
Trust her not,
She is fooling thee!

She has a bosom as white as snow,
Take care!
She knows how much it is best to show,
Beware! Beware!
Trust her not,
She is fooling thee!

She gives thee a garland woven fair,
Take care!

It's a fool's-cap for thee to wear,

Beware! Beware!

Trust her not,

She is fooling thee!

Henry Wadsworth Longfellow.

LOVE IN A COTTAGE

THEY may talk of love in a cottage,
And bowers of trellised vine,—
Of nature bewitchingly simple,
And milkmaids half divine;
They may talk of the pleasure of sleeping
In the shade of a spreading tree,
And a walk in the fields at morning
By the side of a footstep free.

But give me a sly flirtation
By the light of a chandelier,
With music to play in the pauses,
And nobody very near:
Or a seat on a silken sofa,
With a glass of pure old wine,
And mamma too blind to discover
The small white hand in mine.

Your love in a cottage is hungry,
Your vine is a nest for flies,
Your milkmaid shocks the Graces,
And simplicity talks of pies.
You lie down to your shady slumber
And wake with a bug in your ear,
And your damsel that walks in the morning
Is shod like a mountaineer.

True love is at home on a carpet,
And mightily likes his ease,
And true love has an eye for a dinner,

And starves beneath shady trees.
His wing is the fan of a lady,
His foot's an invisible thing,
And his arrow is tipped with a jewel
And shot from a silver string.

Nathaniel Parker Willis.

BECAUSE

SWEET Nea! for your lovely sake
I weave these rambling numbers,
Because I've lain an hour awake,
And can't compose my slumbers;
Because your beauty's gentle light
Is round my pillow beaming,
And flings, I know not why, to-night,
Some witchery o'er my dreaming.

Because we've pass'd some joyous days,
And danced some merry dances;
Because we love old Beaumont's plays,
And old Froissart's romances!
Because whene'er I hear your words
Some pleasant feeling lingers;
Because I think your heart has chords,
That vibrate to your fingers!

Because you've got those long, soft curls,
I've sworn should deck my goddess;
Because you're not like other girls,
All bustle, blush, and bodice!
Because your eyes are deep and blue,
Your fingers long and rosy;
Because a little child and you
Would make one's home so cosy!

Because your little tiny nose
Turns up so pert and funny;
Because I know you choose your beaux

More for their mirth than money;
Because I think you'd rather twirl
A waltz, with me to guide you,
Than talk small nonsense with an earl
And a coronet beside you!

Because you don't object to walk,
And are not given to fainting;
Because you have not learnt to talk
Of flowers, and Poonah-painting;
Because I think you'd scarce refuse
To sew one on a button;
Because I know you'd sometimes choose
To dine on simple mutton!

Because I think I'm just so weak
As, some of those fine morrows,
To ask you if you'll let me speak
My story—and *my* sorrows;
Because the rest's a simple thing,
A matter quickly over,
A church—a priest—a sigh—a ring—
And a chaise and four to Dover.

Edward Fitzgerald.

LILIAN

AIRY, fairy Lilian,
Flitting, fairy Lilian,
When I ask her if she love me,
Clasps her tiny hand above me,
Laughing all she can;
She'll not tell me if she love me,
Cruel little Lilian.

When my passion seeks
Pleasance in love-sighs,
She, looking through and through me,
Thoroughly to undo me,
Smiling, never speaks:

So innocent-arch, so cunning-simple,
From beneath her gathered wimple
Glancing with black-beaded eyes,
Till the lightning laughters dimple
The baby-roses in her cheeks;
Then away she flies.

Prithee weep, May Lilian!
Gaiety without eclipse
Wearieth me, May Lilian:
Through my very heart it thrilleth,
When from crimson-threaded lips
Silver-treble laughter trilleth:
Prithee weep, May Lilian!
Praying all I can,
If prayers will not hurt thee,

Airy Lilian,

Like a rose-leaf I will crush thee,

Fairy Lilian.

Alfred Tennyson.

THE HENCHMAN

MY lady walks her morning round,
My lady's page her fleet greyhound,
My lady's hair the fond winds stir,
And all the birds make songs for her.

Her thrushes sing in Rathburn bowers,
And Rathburn side is gay with flowers;
But ne'er like hers, in flower or bird,
Was beauty seen or music heard.

The distance of the stars is hers;
The least of all her worshippers,
The dust beneath her dainty heel,
She knows not that I see or feel.

Oh, proud and calm!—she cannot know
Where'er she goes with her I go;
Oh, cold and fair!—she cannot guess
I kneel to share her hound's caress!

Gay knights beside her hunt and hawk,
I rob their ears of her sweet talk;
Her suitors come from East and West,
I steal her smiles from every guest.

Unheard of her, in loving words,
I greet her with the song of birds;
I reach her with the green-armed bowers,
I kiss her with the lips of flowers.

The hound and I are on her trail,
The wind and I uplift her veil;

As if the calm, cold moon she were,
And I the tide, I follow her.

As unrebuked as they, I share
The license of the sun and air,
And in a common homage hide
My worship from her scorn and pride.

World-wide apart, and yet so near,
I breathe her charmed atmosphere,
Wherein to her my service brings
The reverence due to holy things.

Her maiden pride, her haughty name,
My dumb devotion shall not shame;
The love that no return doth crave
To knightly levels lifts the slave.

No lance have I, in joust or fight,
To splinter in my lady's sight;
But, at her feet, how blest were I
For any need of hers to die!

John Greenleaf Whittier.

DOROTHY Q
A FAMILY PORTRAIT

GRANDMOTHER'S mother: her age, I guess,
Thirteen summers, or something less;
Girlish bust but womanly air;
Smooth, square forehead with uprolled hair;
Lips that lover has never kissed;
Taper fingers and slender wrist;
Hanging sleeves of stiff brocade;
So they painted the little maid.

On her hand a parrot green
Sits unmoving and broods serene.
Hold up the canvas full in view,—
Look! there's a rent the light shines through,
Dark with a century's fringe of dust,—
That was a Red-Coat's rapier-thrust!
Such is the tale the lady old,
Dorothy's daughter's daughter told.

Who the painter was none may tell,—
One whose best was not over well;
Hard and dry, it must be confessed,
Flat as a rose that has long been pressed;
Yet in her cheek the hues are bright,
Dainty colors of red and white,
And in her slender shape are seen
Hint and promise of stately mien.

Look not on her with eyes of scorn,—
Dorothy Q. was a lady born!

Ay! Since the galloping Normans came,
England's annals have known her name;
And still to the three-hilled rebel town
Dear is that ancient name's renown,
For many a civic wreath they won,
The youthful sire and the gray-haired son.

O Damsel Dorothy! Dorothy Q.!
Strange is the gift that I owe to you;
Such a gift as never a king
Save to daughter or son might bring,—
All my tenure of heart and hand,
All my title to house and land;
Mother and sister and child and wife
And joy and sorrow and death and life!

What if a hundred years ago
Those close-shut lips had answered No,
When forth the tremulous question came
That cost the maiden her Norman name,
And under the folds that look so still
The bodice swelled with the bosom's thrill?
Should I be I, or would it be
One tenth another, to nine tenths me?

Soft is the breath of maiden's Yes:
Not the light gossamer stirs with less;
But never a cable that holds so fast
Through all the battles of wave and blast,
And never an echo of speech or song
That lives in the babbling air so long!

There were tones in the voice that whispered then
You may hear to-day in a hundred men.

O lady and lover, how faint and far
Your images hover,—and here we are,
Solid and stirring in flesh and bone,—
Edward's and Dorothy's—all their own,—
A goodly record for Time to show
Of a syllable spoken so long ago!—
Shall I bless you, Dorothy, or forgive
For the tender whisper that bade me live?

It shall be a blessing, my little maid!
It will heal the stab of the Red-Coat's blade,
And freshen the gold of the tarnished frame,
And gild with a rhyme your household name;
So you shall smile on us brave and bright
As first you greeted the morning's light,
And live untroubled by woes and fears
Through a second youth of a hundred years.

Oliver Wendell Holmes.

A REMINISCENCE

"C'etait en Avril, le Dimanche."—*Pailleron*

'TWAS April; 'twas Sunday; the day was fair,—
Yes! sunny and fair.
And how happy was I!
You wore the white dress you loved to wear;
And two little flowers were hid in your hair—
Yes! in your hair—
On that day—gone by!

We sat on the moss; it was shady and dry;
Yes! shady and dry;
And we sat in the shadow.
We looked at the leaves, we looked at the sky;
We looked at the brook which bubbled near by,—
Yes! bubbled near by,
Through the quiet meadow.

A bird sang on the swinging vine,—
Yes! on the vine,—
And then,—sang not;
I took your little white hand in mine;
'Twas April; 'twas Sunday; 'twas warm sunshine,—
Yes! warm sunshine:
Have you forgot?

James Freeman Clarke.

THE AGE OF WISDOM

HO, pretty page, with the dimpled chin,
That never has known the barber's shear,
All you wish is woman to win,
This is the way that boys begin,—
Wait till you come to Forty Year.

Curly gold locks cover foolish brains,
Billing and cooing is all your cheer;
Sighing and singing of midnight strains,
Under Bonnybell's window panes,—
Wait till you come to Forty Year.

Forty times over let Michaelmas pass,
Grizzling hair the brain doth clear—
Then you know a boy is an ass,
Then you know the worth of a lass,
Once you have come to Forty Year.

Pledge me round, I bid ye declare,
All good fellows whose beards are grey,
Did not the fairest of the fair
Common grow and wearisome ere
Ever a month was passed away?

The reddest lips that ever have kissed,
The brightest eyes that ever have shone,
May pray and whisper, and we not list,
Or look away, and never be missed,
Ere yet ever a month is gone.

Gillian's dead, God rest her bier,

How I loved her twenty years syne!
Marian's married, but I sit here
Alone and merry at Forty Year,
Dipping my nose in the Gascon wine.

William Makepeace Thackeray.

THE BALLAD OF BOUILLABAISSE

A STREET there is in Paris famous,
For which no rhyme our language yields,
Rue Neuve des Petits Champs its name is—
The New Street of the Little Fields.
And here's an inn, not rich and splendid
But still in comfortable case;
The which in youth I oft attended
To eat a bowl of Bouillabaisse.

This Bouillabaisse a noble dish is,
A sort of soup or broth, or brew,
Or hotchpotch of all sorts of fishes
That Greenwich never could outdo;
Green herbs, red peppers, mussels, saffron,
Soles, onions, garlic, roach and dace:
All these you eat at Terrè's tavern
In that one dish of Bouillabaisse.

Indeed a rich and savoury stew 'tis;
And true philosophers, methinks,
Who love all sorts of natural beauties
Should love good victuals and good drinks.
And Cordelier or Benedictine
Might gladly, sure, his lot embrace,
Nor find a fast-day too afflicting
Which served him up a Bouillabaisse.

I wonder if the house still there is?
Yes, here the lamp is, as before;
The smiling red-cheeked "écaillère" is

Still opening oysters at the door.
Is Terrè still alive and able?
I recollect his droll grimace;
He'd come and smile before your table
And hope you liked your Bouillabaisse.

We enter—nothing's changed or older.
"How's Monsieur Terrè, waiter, pray?"
The waiter stares and shrugs his shoulder—
"Monsieur is dead this many a day."
"It is the lot of saint and sinner,
So honest Terrè's run his race."
"What will Monsieur require for dinner?"
"Say, do you still cook Bouillabaisse?"

"Oh, oui, Monsieur," is the waiter's answer,
"Quel vin, Monsieur, désire-t-il?"
"Tell me a good one." "That I can, sir:
The Chambertin with yellow seal."
"So Terrè's gone," I say, and sink in
My old accustom'd corner place;
"He's done with feasting and with drinking,
With Burgundy and Bouillabaisse."

My old accustom'd corner here is,
The table still is in the nook;
Ah! vanish'd many a busy year is;
This well-known chair since last I took,
When first I saw ye, "*cari luoghi*,"
I'd scarce a beard upon my face,
And now a grizzled, grim old fogy,

I sit and wait for Bouillabaisse.

Where are you, old companions trusty
Of early days met here to dine?
Come, waiter! quick, a flagon crusty,
I'll pledge them in the good old wine.
The kind old voices and old faces
My memory can quick retrace;
Around the board they take their places,
And share the wine and Bouillabaisse.

There's Jack has made a wondrous marriage,
There's laughing Tom is laughing yet,
There's brave Augustus drives his carriage,
There's poor old Fred in the "Gazette";
On James's head the grass is growing:
Good Lord! the world has wagged a-pace,
Since here we set the claret flowing
And drank, and ate the Bouillabaisse.

Ah me! how quick the days are flitting.
I mind me of the time that's gone,
When here I'd sit, as now I'm sitting
In this same place—but not alone.
A fair young form was nestled near me,
A dear, dear face looked fondly up,
And sweetly spoke, and smiled to cheer me—
There's no one now to share my cup.

I drink it as the Fates ordain it.
Come, fill it, and have done with rhymes:
Fill up the lonely glass and drain it

In memory of dear old times.
Welcome the wine, whate'er the seal is,
And sit you down and say your grace
With thankful heart whate'er the meat is.
—Here comes the smoking Bouillabaisse!

William Makepeace Thackeray.

AN INVITATION

TELL me, pretty one, where will you sail?
How shall our bark be steered, I pray?
Breezes flutter each silken veil,
Tell me, where will you go to-day?

My vessel's helm is of ivory white,
Her bulwarks glisten with jewels bright
And red gold;
The sails are made from the wings of a dove,
And the man at the wheel is the god of love,
Blithe and bold.

Where shall we sail? 'Mid the Baltic's foam?
Or over the broad Pacific roam?
Don't refuse.
Say, shall we gather the sweet snow-flowers,
Or wander in rose-strewn Eastern bowers?
Only choose.

"Oh, carry me then," cried the fair coquette,
"To the land where never I've journeyed yet,
To that shore
Where love is lasting, and change unknown,
And a man is faithful to one alone
Evermore."

Go, seek that land for a year and a day,
At the end of the time you'll be still far away
Pretty maid;—
'Tis a country unlettered in map or in chart,

'Tis a country that does not exist, sweetheart,
I'm afraid!

Translated from Théophile Gautier.

FANNY; OR THE BEAUTY AND THE BEE

FANNY, array'd in the bloom of her beauty,
Stood at the mirror, and toy'd with her hair,
Viewing her charms, till she felt it a duty
To own that like Fanny no woman was fair.
A Bee from the garden—oh, what could mislead him?—
Stray'd through the lattice new dainties to seek,
And lighting on Fanny, too busy to heed him,
Stung the sweet maid on her delicate cheek.

Smarting with pain, round the chamber she sought him,
Tears in her eyes, and revenge in her heart,
And angrily cried, when at length she had caught him,
"Die for the deed, little wretch that thou art!"
Stooping to crush him, the hapless offender
Pray'd her for mercy,—to hear and forgive;
"Oh, spare me!" cried he, "by those eyes in their splendour;
Oh, pity my fault, and allow me to live!

"Am I to blame that your cheeks are like roses,
Whose hues all the pride of the garden eclipse?
Lilies are hid in your mouth when it closes,
And odours of Araby breathe from your lips."
Sweet Fanny relented: "'twere cruel to hurt you;
Small is the fault, pretty bee, you deplore;
And e'en were it greater, forgiveness is virtue;
Go forth and be happy—I blame you no more."

Charles Mackay.

GARDEN FANCIES
THE FLOWER'S NAME

I

HERE'S the garden she walked across,
Arm in my arm, such a short while since:
Hark, now I push its wicket, the moss
Hinders the hinges and makes them wince!
She must have reached this shrub ere she turned,
As back with that murmur the wicket swung;
For she laid the poor snail, my chance foot spurned,
To feed and forget it the leaves among.

II

Down this side of the gravel-walk
She went while her robe's edge brushed the box:
And here she paused in her gracious talk
To point me a moth on the milk-white phlox.
Roses ranged in a valiant row,
I will never think that she passed you by!
She loves you, noble roses, I know;
But yonder, see, where the rock-plants lie!

III

This flower she stooped at, finger on lip,
Stooped over in doubt, as settling its claim;
Till she gave me, with pride to make no slip,
Its soft meandering Spanish name:
What a name! Was it love or praise?
Speech half-asleep or song half-awake?

I must learn Spanish, one of these days,
Only for that slow sweet name's sake.

IV

Roses, if I live and do well,
I may bring her, one of these days,
To fix you fast with as fine a spell,
Fit you each with his Spanish phrase;
But do not detain me now; for she lingers
There, like sunshine over the ground,
And ever I see her soft white fingers
Searching after the bud she found.

V

Flower, you Spaniard, look that you grow not,
Stay as you are and be loved for ever!
Bud, if I kiss you, 'tis that you blow not:
Mind, the shut pink mouth opens never!
For while it pouts, her fingers wrestle
Twinkling the audacious leaves between,
Till round they turn and down they nestle—
Is not the dear mark still to be seen?

VI

Where I find her not, beauties vanish;
Whither I follow her, beauties flee;
Is there no method to tell her in Spanish
June's twice June since she breathed it with me?
Come, bud, show me the least of her traces,
Treasure my lady's lightest footfall!

—Ah, you may flout and turn up your faces—
Roses, you are not so fair after all!

Robert Browning.

A POEM OF EVERY-DAY LIFE

HE tore him from the merry throng
Within the billiard hall;
He was gotten up regardlessly
To pay his party call.
His thoughts were dire and dark within,
Discourteous to fate:
"Ah, me! these social debts incurred
Are hard to liquidate."

His boots were slender, long and trim;
His collar tall and swell;
His hats were made by Dunlap,
And his coats were cut by Bell;
A symphony in black and white,
"Of our set" the pride,
Yet he lingered on his way—
He would that he had died.

His feet caressed the lonely way,
The pave gave forth no sound;
They seemed in pitying silence clothed
West-End-ward he was bound.
He approached the mansion stealthily,
The step looked cold and chill;
He glanced into the vestibule,
But all was calm and still.

He fingered nervously the bell,
His card-case in his hand;
He saw the mirror in the hall—

Solemn, stately, grand.
Suddenly his spirits rose;
The drawing-room looked dim;
The menial filled his soul with joy
With "No, there's no one in."

With fiendish glee he stole away;
His heart was gay and light,
Happy that he went and paid
His party call that night.
His steps turned to the billiard hall,
Blissfully he trod;
He entered: "What, returned so soon?"
Replied: "She's out, thank God!"

Sixteen cues were put to rest
Within their upright beds,
And sixteen different tiles were placed
On sixteen level heads;
Sixteen men upon the street
In solid phalanx all,
And sixteen men on duty bent
To pay their party call.

When the fairest of her sex came home
At early dawn, I ween,
She slowly looked the cards all out—
They numbered seventeen.
With calm relief she raised her eyes,
Filled with grateful light,
"Oh, merciful Fate, look down and see

What I've escaped this night!"

Albert Riddle.

LOVE DISPOSED OF

HERE goes Love! Now cut him clear,
A weight about his neck:
If he linger longer here,
Our ship will be a wreck.
Overboard! Overboard!
Down let him go!
In the deep he may sleep
Where the corals grow.

He said he'd woo the gentle breeze,
A bright tear in her eye;
But she was false or hard to please,
Or he has told a lie.
Overboard! overboard!
Down in the sea
He may find a truer mind,
Where the mermaids be.

He sang us many a merry song
While the breeze was kind;
But he has been lamenting long
The falseness of the wind.
Overboard! overboard!
Under the wave
Let him sing where smooth shells ring
In the ocean's cave.

He may struggle; he may weep;
We'll be stern and cold;
His grief will find, within the deep,

More tears than can be told.

He has gone overboard!

We will float on;

We shall find a truer wind,

Now that he is gone.

Robert Traill Spence Lowell.

MABEL, IN NEW HAMPSHIRE

FAIREST of the fairest, rival of the rose,
That is Mabel of the Hills, as everybody knows.

Do you ask me near what stream this sweet floweret grows?
That's an ignorant question, sir, as everybody knows.

Ask you what her age is, reckoned as time goes?
Just the age of beauty, as everybody knows.

Is she tall as Rosalind, standing on her toes?
She is just the perfect height, as everybody knows.

What's the color of her eyes, when they ope or close?
Just the color they should be, as everybody knows.

Is she lovelier dancing, or resting in repose?
Both are radiant pictures, as everybody knows.

Do her ships go sailing on every wind that blows?
She is richer far than that, as everybody knows.

Has she scores of lovers, heaps of bleeding beaux?
That question's quite superfluous, as everybody knows.

I could tell you something, if I only chose!—
But what's the use of telling what everybody knows?

James Thomas Fields.

THE COQUETTE
A PORTRAIT

"YOU'RE clever at drawing, I own,"
Said my beautiful cousin Lisette,
As we sat by the window alone,
"But say, can you paint a Coquette?"

"She's painted already," quoth I;
"Nay, nay!" said the laughing Lisette,
"Now none of your joking—but try
And paint me a thorough Coquette."

"Well, Cousin," at once I began
In the ear of the eager Lisette,
"I'll paint you as well as I can,
That wonderful thing, a Coquette.

"She wears a most beautiful face"
("Of course," said the pretty Lisette),
"And isn't deficient in grace,
Or else she were not a Coquette.

"And then she is daintily made"
(A smile from the dainty Lisette)
"By people expert in the trade
Of forming a proper Coquette.

"She's the winningest ways with the beaux"
("Go on!" said the winning Lisette),
"But there isn't a man of them knows
The mind of the fickle Coquette!

"She knows how to weep and to sigh"

(A sigh from the tender Lisette),
"But her weeping is all in my eye—
Not that of the cunning Coquette!

"In short, she's a creature of art"
("Oh, hush!" said the frowning Lisette),
"With merely the ghost of a heart—
Enough for a thorough Coquette.

"And yet I could easily prove"
("Now don't!" said the angry Lisette),
"The lady is always in love—
In love with herself—the Coquette!

"There—do not be angry—you know,
My dear little Cousin Lisette,
You told me a moment ago,
To paint you—a thorough Coquette!"

John Godfrey Saxe.

JUSTINE, YOU LOVE ME NOT!

"Helas! vous ne m'aimez pas."—Piron.

I know, Justine, you speak me fair
As often as we meet;
And 'tis a luxury, I swear,
To hear a voice so sweet;
And yet it does not please me quite,
The civil way you've got;
For me you're something too polite—
Justine, you love me not!

I know, Justine, you never scold
At aught that I may do:
If I am passionate or cold,
'Tis all the same to you.
"A charming temper," say the men,
"To smooth a husband's lot":
I wish 'twere ruffled now and then—
Justine, you love me not!

I know, Justine, you wear a smile
As beaming as the sun;
But who supposes all the while
It shines for only one?
Though azure skies are fair to see,
A transient cloudy spot
In yours would promise more to me—
Justine, you love me not!

I know, Justine, you make my name

Your eulogistic theme,
And say—if any chance to blame—
You hold me in esteem.
Such words, for all their kindly scope,
Delight me not a jot;
Just as you would have praised the Pope—
Justine, you love me not!

I know, Justine—for I have heard
What friendly voices tell—
You do not blush to say the word,
"You like me passing well;"
And thus the fatal sound I hear
That seals my lonely lot:
There's nothing now to hope or fear—
Justine, you love me not!

John Godfrey Saxe.

SING HEIGH-HO!

THERE sits a bird on every tree
Sing heigh-ho!
There sits a bird on every tree,
And courts his love, as I do thee;
Sing heigh-ho, and heigh-ho!
Young maids must marry.

There grows a flower on every bough,
Sing heigh-ho!
There grows a flower on every bough,
Its petals kiss—I'll show you how:
Sing heigh-ho and heigh-ho!
Young maids must marry.

From sea to stream the salmon roam:
Sing heigh-ho!
From sea to stream the salmon roam;
Each finds a mate, and leads her home;
Sing heigh-ho, and heigh-ho!
Young maids must marry.

The sun's a bridegroom, earth a bride,
Sing heigh-ho!
They court from morn till eventide:
The earth shall pass, but love abide;
Sing heigh-ho, and heigh-ho!
Young maids must marry.

Charles Kingsley.

SNOWDROP

WHEN, full of warm and eager love,
I clasp you in my fond embrace,
You gently push me back and say,
"Take care, my dear, you'll spoil my lace."

You kiss me just as you would kiss
Some woman friend you chanced to see;
You call me "dearest."—All love's forms
Are yours, not its reality.

Oh, Annie! cry, and storm, and rave!
Do anything with passion in it!
Hate me an hour, and then turn round
And love me truly, just one minute.

William Wetmore Story.

THE PROTEST

I COULD not bear to see those eyes
On all with wasteful largess shine,
And that delight of welcome rise
Like sunshine strained through amber wine,
But that a glow from deeper skies,
From conscious fountains more divine,
Is (is it?) mine.

Be beautiful to all mankind,
As Nature fashioned thee to be;
'Twould anger me did all not find
The sweet perfection that's in thee;
Yet keep one charm of charms behind,—
Nay, thou 'rt so rich, keep two of three
For (is it?) me!

James Russell Lowell.

SCHERZO

WHEN the down is on the chin
And the gold-gleam in the hair,
When the birds their sweethearts win
And champagne is in the air
Love is here, and Love is there,
Love is welcome everywhere.

Summer's cheek too soon turns thin,
Day grows briefer, sunshine rare;
Autumn from his cannikin
Blows the froth to chase Despair:
Love is met with frosty stare,
Cannot house 'neath branches bare.

When new life is in the leaf
And new red is in the rose,
Though Love's Maytime be as brief
As a dragon-fly's repose,
Never moments come like those,
Be they Heaven or Hell: who knows?

All too soon comes Winter's grief,
Spendthrift Love's false friends turn foes;
Softly comes Old Age, the thief,
Steals the rapture, leaves the throes:
Love his mantle round him throws,—
"Time to say good-bye; it snows."

James Russell Lowell.

THE HANDSOMEST MAN IN THE ROOM

I'VE always been told that I'm pretty
(And really I think so myself),
I'm accomplished, good-tempered, and witty,
And papa has got plenty of pelf.
My teeth, eyes, and curls, I won't mention,
My shape, nor my delicate bloom;
But I'm sure I deserve the attention
Of "the handsomest man in the room."
Yes, I know I deserve the attention,
Of the "handsomest man in the room."

When I met that sublimest of fellows,
The sight really made my heart jump;
Other men shrank to mere punchinellos,
As he towered like a pine in a clump.
So noble and classic each feature,
With a touching expression of gloom,
That I said to myself—"The dear creature!
He's the handsomest man in the room!"
"Yes!" I said to myself,—"The dear creature!
He's the handsomest man in the room!"

He asked me if I'd walk a measure,
(When he came it was nearly midnight)—
I said—"With a great deal of pleasure,"
For he danced like a perfect delight.
So in waltzing and polking we sported,
Till supper sent forth its perfume,
And I went down to table, escorted

By "the handsomest man in the room"—
Yes, I went down to table, escorted
By "the handsomest man in the room."

I thought 'twas a nice situation,
So snugly together we sat,
And in hopes of a pleasant flirtation,
I tried to engage him in chat.
But, to talk of himself never backward,
He strove modest airs to assume,
For he told me, he felt very awkward
As "the handsomest man in the room"—
Really, really, one does feel so awkward,
As "the handsomest man in the room!"

Thought I—"This is really too stupid!
Your good looks are very well known,
But you ought to know, Grenadier Cupid,
That I'd much rather hear of my own."
Yet should he reform in this one thing
(Of which there are hopes, I presume),
We still may contrive to make something
Of the handsomest man in the room,
Yes, we still may contrive to make something
Of the handsomest man in the room.

William Macquorn Rankine.

THE LAWYER'S INVOCATION TO SPRING

WHEREAS, on certain boughs and sprays
Now divers birds are heard to sing,
And sundry flowers their heads upraise,
Hail to the coming on of Spring!

The songs of those said birds arouse
The memory of our youthful hours,
As green as those said sprays and boughs,
As fresh and sweet as those said flowers.

The birds aforesaid—happy pairs—
Love, 'mid the aforesaid boughs, inshrines
In freehold nests; themselves their heirs,
Administrators, and assigns.

O busiest term of Cupid's Court,
Where tender plaintiffs actions bring,—
Season of frolic and of sport,
Hail, as aforesaid, coming Spring!

Henry Howard Brownell.

A TERRIBLE INFANT

I RECOLLECT a nurse call'd Ann
Who carried me about the grass,
And one fine day a fine young man
Came up and kiss'd the pretty lass.
She did not make the least objection!
Thinks I, "Aha!
When I can talk I'll tell Mamma"—
And that's my earliest recollection.

Frederick Locker-Lampson.

LOULOU AND HER CAT

GOOD pastry is vended
In Cité Fadette;
Maison Pons can make splendid
Brioche and *galette*.

M'sieu Pons is so fat that
He's laid on the shelf;
Madame had a Cat that
Was fat as herself.

Long hair, soft as satin,
A musical purr,
'Gainst the window she'd flatten
Her delicate fur.

I drove Lou to see what
Our neighbours were at,
In rapture, cried she, "What
An exquisite cat!

"What whiskers! She's purring
All over. Regale
Our eyes, *Puss*, by stirring
Thy feathery tail!

"*M'sieu Pons*, will you sell her?"
"*Ma femme est sortie*,
Your offer I'll tell her;
But will she?" says he.

Yet *Pons* was persuaded
To part with the prize:

(Our bargain was aided,
My Lou, by your eyes!)

From his *légitime* save him,—
My spouse I prefer,
For I warrant *his* gave him
Un mauvais quart d'heure.

I am giving a pleasant
Grimalkin to Lou,
—Ah, *Puss*, what a present
I'm giving to you!

Frederick Locker-Lampson.

PICCADILLY

PICCADILLY! Shops, palaces, bustle, and breeze,
The whirring of wheels, and the murmur of trees;
By night or by day, whether noisy or stilly,
Whatever my mood is, I love Piccadilly.

Wet nights, when the gas on the pavement is streaming,
And young Love is watching, and old Love is dreaming,
And Beauty is whirling to conquest, where shrilly
Cremona makes nimble thy toes, Piccadilly!

Bright days, when a stroll is my afternoon wont
And I meet all the people I do know, or don't:
Here is jolly old Brown, and his fair daughter Lillie—
No wonder, young Pilgrim, you like Piccadilly!

See yonder pair riding, how fondly they saunter,
She smiles on her poet, whose heart's in a canter!
Some envy her spouse, and some covet her filly,
He envies them both,—he's an ass, Piccadilly!

Now were I such a bride, with a slave at my feet,
I would choose me a house in my favourite street;
Yes or no—I would carry my point, willy-nilly:
If "no,"—pick a quarrel; if "yes"—Piccadilly!

From Primrose balcony, long ages ago,
"Old Q." sat at gaze,—who now passes below?
A frolicsome statesman, the Man of the Day
A laughing philosopher, gallant and gay;

Never darling of fortune more manfully trod,
Full of years, full of fame, and the world at his nod,

Can the thought reach his heart, and then leave it more chilly—
Old P. or old Q.,—"I must quit Piccadilly?"

Life is chequer'd; a patchwork of smiles and of frowns;
We value its ups, let us muse on its downs;
There's a side that is bright, it will then turn us t'other,
One turn, if a good one, deserves yet another.
These downs are delightful, these ups are not hilly,—
Let us try one more turn ere we quit Piccadilly.

Frederick Locker-Lampson.

A WORD THAT MAKES US LINGER

(Written in the visitor's book at Gopsall)

KIND hostess mine, who raised the latch
And welcomed me beneath your thatch,
Who makes me here forget the pain,
And all the pleasures of Cockaigne,
Now, pen in hand, and pierced with woe,
I write one word before I go—
A word that dies upon my lips
While thus you kiss your finger-tips.

When Black-eyed Sue was rowed to land
That word she cried, and waved her hand—
Her lily hand!
It seems absurd,
But I can't write that dreadful word.

Frederick Locker-Lampson.

MY MISTRESS'S BOOTS

THEY nearly strike me dumb,
And I tremble when they come
Pit-a-pat:
This palpitation means
That these Boots are Geraldine's—
Think of that!

Oh where did hunter win
So delectable a skin
For her feet?
You lucky little kid,
You perish'd, so you did,
For my sweet!

The faery stitching gleams
On the sides, and in the seams,
And it shows
That the Pixies were the wags
Who tipt these funny tags,
And these toes.

The simpletons who squeeze
Their extremities to please
Mandarins,
Would positively flinch
From venturing to pinch
Geraldine's.

What soles to charm an elf!
Had Crusoe, sick of self,

Chanced to view
One printed near the tide,
Oh how hard he would have tried
For the two!

For Gerry's debonair,
And innocent and fair
As a rose:
She's an angel in a frock,
With a fascinating cock
To her nose.

Cinderella's lefts and rights
To Geraldine's were frights;
And, I trow,
The damsel, deftly shod,
Has dutifully trod
Until now.

Come, Gerry, since it suits
Such a pretty Puss (in Boots)
These to don,
Set this dainty hand awhile
On my shoulder, dear, and I'll
Put them on.

Frederick Locker-Lampson.

A NICE CORRESPONDENT!

THE glow and the glory are plighted
To darkness, for evening is come;
The lamp in Glebe Cottage is lighted,
The birds and the sheep-bells are dumb.
I'm alone in my casement, for Pappy
Is summon'd to dinner at Kew:
I'm alone, dearest Fred, but I'm happy—
I'm thinking of you!

I wish you were here! Were I duller
Than dull, you'd be dearer than dear;
I'm drest in your favourite colour—
Dear Fred, how I wish you were here!
I am wearing my lazuli necklace,
The necklace you fasten'd askew!
Was there ever so rude and so reckless
A darling as you?

I want you to come and pass sentence
On two or three books with a plot;
Of course you know "Janet's Repentance"?
I'm reading Sir Waverley Scott,
The story of Edgar and Lucy,
How thrilling, romantic, and true!
The master (his bride was a goosey!)
Reminds me of you.

They tell me Cockaigne has been crowning
A Poet whose garland endures;
It was you who first spouted me Browning,—

That stupid old Browning of yours!
His vogue and his verve are alarming,
I'm anxious to give him his due,
But, Fred, he's not nearly so charming
A Poet as you!

I heard how you shot at the Beeches,
I saw how you rode Chanticleer,
I have read the report of your speeches,
And echoed the echoing cheer.
There's a whisper of hearts you are breaking,
Dear Fred, I believe it, I do!
Small marvel that Fashion is making
Her idol of you!

Alas for the world, and its dearly
Bought triumph, its fugitive bliss;
Sometimes I half wish I was merely
A plain or a penniless miss;
But perhaps one is best with "a measure
Of pelf," and I'm not sorry, too,
That I'm pretty, because 'tis a pleasure,
My darling, to you!

Your whim is for frolic and fashion,
Your taste is for letters and art;—
This rhyme is the commonplace passion
That glows in a fond woman's heart:
Lay it by in a dainty deposit
For relics—we all have a few!
Love, some day they'll print it, because it

Was written to you!

Frederick Locker-Lampson.

THERE'S A TIME TO BE JOLLY

THERE'S a time to be jolly, a time to repent,
A season for folly, a season for Lent,
The first as the worst we too often regard;
The rest as the best, but our judgment is hard.

There are snows in December and Roses in June,
There's darkness at midnight and sunshine at noon;
But, were there no sorrow, no storm-cloud or rain,
Who'd care for the morrow with beauty again.

The world is a picture both gloomy and bright,
And grief is the shadow and pleasure the light,
And neither should smother the general tone:
For where were the other if either were gone?

The valley is lovely; the mountain is drear,
Its summit is hidden in mist all the year;
But gaze from the heaven, high over all weather,
And mountain and valley are lovely together.

I have learned to love Lucy, though faded she be;
If my next love be lovely, the better for me.
By the end of next summer, I'll give you my oath,
It was best, after all, to have flirted with both.

Charles Godfrey Leland.

I REMEMBER, I REMEMBER

I REMEMBER, I remember,
The house where I was wed,
And the little room from which, that night,
My smiling bride was led;
She didn't come a wink too soon,
Nor make too long a stay;
But now I often wish her folks
Had kept the girl away!

I remember, I remember,
Her dresses, red and white,
Her bonnets and her caps and cloaks,—
They cost an awful sight!
The "corner lot" on which I built,
And where my brother met
At first my wife, one washing-day,—
That man is single yet!

I remember, I remember,
Where I was used to court,
And thought that all of married life
Was just such pleasant sport:
My spirit flew in feathers then,
No care was on my brow;
I scarce could wait to shut the gate,—
I'm not so anxious now!

I remember, I remember,
My dear one's smile and sigh;
I used to think her tender heart

Was close against the sky;
It was a childish ignorance,
But now it soothes me not
To know I'm farther off from heaven
Than when she wasn't got!

Phœbe Cary.

THE FLOWER OF LOVE LIES BLEEDING

I MET a little maid one day,
All in the bright May weather;
She danced, and brushed the dew away
As lightly as a feather.
She had a ballad in her hand
That she had just been reading,
But was too young to understand:—
That ditty of a distant land,
"The flower of love lies bleeding."

She tripped across the meadow grass,
To where a brook was flowing,
Across the brook like wind did pass,—
Wherever flowers were growing
Like some bewildered child she flew,
Whom fairies were misleading:
"Whose butterfly," I said, "are you?
And what sweet thing do you pursue?"—
"The flower of love lies bleeding!"

"I've found the wild rose in the hedge,
I've found the tiger-lily,—
The blue flag by the water's edge,—
The dancing daffodilly,—
King-cups and pansies,—every flower
Except the one I'm needing;—
Perhaps it grows in some dark bower,
And opens at a later hour,—
This flower of love lies bleeding."

"I wouldn't look for it," I said,
"For you can do without it:
There's no such flower." She shook her head;
"But I have read about it!"
I talked to her of bee and bird,
But she was all unheeding:
Her tender heart was strangely stirred,
She harped on that unhappy word,—
"The flower of love lies bleeding!"

"My child," I sighed, and dropped a tear,
"I would no longer mind it;
You'll find it some day, never fear,
For all of us must find it!
I found it many a year ago,
With one of gentle breeding;
You and the little lad you know,—
I see why you are weeping so,—
Your flower of love lies bleeding!"

Richard Henry Stoddard.

THE GOLD ROOM
AN IDYL

THEY come from mansions far up-town,
And from their country villas,
And some, Charybdis' gulf whirls down,
And some fall into Scylla's.
Lo! here young Paris climbs the stairs
As if their slope were Ida's,
And here his golden touch declares
The ass's ears of Midas.

It seems a Bacchic, brawling rout
To every business-scorner,
But such, methinks, must be an "out,"
Or has not made a "corner."
In me the rhythmic gush revives;
I feel a classic passion:
We, also, lead Arcadian lives,
Though in a Broad-Street fashion.

Old Battos, here, 's a leading bull,
And Diomed a bear is,
And near them, shearing bankers' wool,
Strides the Tiltonian Charis;
And Atys, there, has gone to smash,
His every bill protested,
While Cleon's eyes with comfort flash,—
I have his funds invested!

Mehercle! 'tis the same thing yet
As in the days of Pindar:

The Isthmian race, the dust and sweat,
The prize—why, what's to hinder?
And if I twang my lyre at times,
They did so then, I reckon;
That man's the best at modern rhymes
Whom you can draw a check on!

Bayard Taylor.

COMFORT

WHO would care to pass his life away
Of the Lotos-land a dreamful denizen,—
Lotos-islands in a waveless bay,
Sung by Alfred Tennyson?

Who would care to be a dull new-comer
Far across the wild sea's wide abysses,
Where, about the earth's three thousandth summer,
Passed divine Ulysses?

Rather give me coffee, art, a book,
From my windows a delicious sea-view,
Southdown mutton, somebody to cook,—
"Music?"—I believe you.

Strawberry icebergs in the summer time,—
But of elm-wood many a massive splinter,
Good ghost stories, and a classic rhyme,
For the nights of winter.

Now and then a friend and some Sauterne,
Now and then a haunch of Highland venison,
And for Lotos-land I'll never yearn,
Malgré Alfred Tennyson.

Mortimer Collins.

A SUMMER SONG

SUMMER is sweet, ay! summer is sweet,—
Minna mine with the brown, brown eyes:
Red are the roses under his feet,
Clear the blue of his windless skies.
Pleasant it is in a boat to glide
On a river whose ripples to ocean haste,
With indolent fingers fretting the tide,
And an indolent arm round a darling waist—
And to see as the Western purple dies,
Hesper mirrored in brown, brown eyes.

Summer is fleet, ah! summer is fleet,—
Minna mine with the brown, brown eyes:
Onward travel his flying feet,
And the mystical colours of autumn rise.
Clouds will gather round evening star—
Sorrow may silence our first gay rhyme,—
The river's swift ripples flow tardier far
Than the golden minutes of love's sweet time:
But to me, whom omnipotent love makes wise,
There's endless summer in brown, brown eyes.

Mortimer Collins.

MY AUNT'S SPECTRE

THEY tell me (but I really can't
Imagine such a rum thing),
It is the phantom of my Aunt,
Who ran away—or something.

It is the very worst of bores:
(My Aunt was most delightful).
It prowls about the corridors,
And utters noises frightful.

At midnight through the rooms It glides,
Behaving very coolly,
Our hearts all throb against our sides—
The lights are burning bluely.

The lady, in her living hours,
Was the most charming vixen
That ever this poor sex of ours
Delighted to play tricks on.

Yes, that's her portrait on the wall,
In quaint old-fangled bodice:
Her eyes are blue—her waist is small—
A ghost! Pooh, pooh,—a goddess!

A fine patrician shape, to suit
My dear old father's sister—
Lips softly curved, a dainty foot:
Happy the man that kissed her!

Light hair of crisp irregular curl
Over fair shoulders scattered—

Egad, she was a pretty girl,
Unless Sir Thomas flattered!

And who the deuce, in these bright days,
Could possibly expect her
To take to dissipated ways
And plague us as a spectre?

Mortimer Collins.

A CONCEIT

OH, touch that rose-bud! it will bloom—
My lady fair!
A passionate red in dim green gloom,
A joy, a splendor, a perfume
That sleeps in air.

You touched my heart; it gave a thrill
Just like a rose
That opens at a lady's will;
Its bloom is always yours, until
You bid it close.

Mortimer Collins.

MARTIAL IN LONDON

EXQUISITE wines and comestibles,
From Slater, and Fortnum and Mason;
Billiard, écarté, and chess tables;
Water in vast marble basin;
Luminous books (not voluminous)
To read under beech-trees cacuminous;
One friend, who is fond of a distich,
And doesn't get too syllogistic;
A valet, who knows the complete art
Of service—a maiden, his sweetheart:
Give me these, in some rural pavilion,
And I'll envy no Rothschild his million.

Mortimer Collins.

THE BEST OF THE BALL

AT last! O, sensation delicious!
At last, it is here, it is here!
That moment supremely auspicious
In the jolliest ball of the year.

It is all as I dreamt it would happen—
The rooms grown oppressive with heat,
And my darling, alarm'd with the crowding,
Suggesting a timely retreat.

"Not there; not among the exotics;
I faint with that fragrance of theirs.
Let us go—it will be so refreshing—
And find out a seat on the stairs."

How dear are the lips that could utter
Such exquisite music as this!
How I listen'd, my heart all a-flutter,
Assenting, transported with bliss!

All the house with the dancers is throbbing,
The music seems born of the air:
O, joy of all joy the extremest,
To sit, as I sit, on a stair!

To sit, and to gaze on my darling,
Enraptured in thrilling delight,
As I think, "Never face could be fairer,
Nor eyes half so tenderly bright."

It is all as I knew it would happen,
Yet, no; there is something I miss—

The eloquent words I intended
To speak in a moment like this.

They were tender, and soft, and poetic,
And I thought, "As I timidly speak,
She will smile, and a blush sympathetic
Will crimson the rose in her cheek."

And now that we sit here together,
I only—do all that I can—
Converse on the ball and the weather,
While she opens and closes her fan.

What I thought to have said seems audacious,
Her ear it would surely offend;
She would turn from me, no longer gracious,
And frown my delight to an end.

Far better to talk of the weather,
Or ponder in rapture supreme:
'Tis so joyous to sit here together,
So pleasant to wake and to dream!

Contented, long hours we could measure,
Forgetting, forgotten by all;
Nor envy the dancers their pleasure
For ours is the best of the ball.

William Sawyer.

THE BALLAD OF DEAD LADIES

(Translation from François Villon, 1450)

TELL me now in what hidden way is
Lady Flora the lovely Roman?
Where's Hipparchia, and where is Thais,
Neither of them the fairer woman?
Where is Echo, beheld of no man,
Only heard on river and mere,—
She whose beauty was more than human? . . .
But where are the snows of yester-year?

Where's Heloise, the learned nun,
For whose sake Abeillard, I ween,
Lost manhood and put priesthood on?
(From love he won such dule and teen!)
And where, I pray you is the Queen
Who will'd that Buridan should steer
Sew'd in a sack's mouth down the Seine? . . .
But where are the snows of yester-year?

White Queen Blanche, like a queen of lilies,
With a voice like any mermaiden,—
Bertha Broadfoot, Beatrice, Alice,
And Ermengarde the lady of Maine,—
And that good Joan whom Englishmen
At Rouen doom'd and burn'd her there,—
Mother of God, Where are they then? . . .
But where are the snows of yester-year?

Nay, never ask this weak, fair lord,

Where they are gone, nor yet this year,
Save with thus much for an overword,—
But where are the snows of yester-year?

Dante Gabriel Rossetti.

FEMININE ARITHMETIC

Laura

ON me he shall ne'er put a ring,
So, mamma, 'tis in vain to take trouble—
For I was but eighteen in spring,
While his age exactly is double.

Mamma

He's but in his thirty-sixth year,
Tall, handsome, good-natured and witty,
And should you refuse him, my dear,
May you die an old maid without pity!

Laura

His figure, I grant you, will pass,
And at present he's young enough plenty;
But when I am sixty, alas!
Will not he be a hundred and twenty?

Charles Graham Halpine.

A TRIFLE

I KNOW not why, but ev'n to me
My songs seem sweet when read to thee.

Perhaps in this the pleasure lies—
I read my thoughts within thine eyes.

And so dare fancy that my art
May sink as deeply as thy heart.

Perhaps I love to make my words
Sing round thee like so many birds,

Or, Maybe, they are only sweet
As they seem offerings at thy feet.

Or haply, Lily, when I speak,
I think, perchance, they touch thy cheek,

Or with a yet more precious bliss,
Die on thy red lips in a kiss.

Each reason here—I cannot tell—
Or all perhaps may solve the spell.

But if she watch when I am by,
Lily may deeper see than I.

Henry Timrod.

FLIGHT

O MEMORY! that which I gave thee
To guard in thy garner yestreen—
Little deeming thou e'er could'st behave thee
Thus basely—hath gone from thee clean!
Gone, fled, as ere autumn is ended
The yellow leaves flee from the oak—
I have lost it forever, my splendid
Original joke.

What was it? I know I was brushing
My hair when the notion occurred:
I know that I felt myself blushing
As I thought, "How supremely absurd!
How they'll hammer on floor and on table
As its drollery dawns on them—how
They will quote it"—I wish I were able
To quote it just now.

I had thought to lead up conversation
To the subject—it's easily done—
Then let off, as an airy creation
Of the moment, that masterly pun.
Let it off, with a flash like a rocket's;
In the midst of a dazzled conclave,
Where I sat, with my hands in my pockets,
The only one grave.

I had fancied young Titterton's chuckles,
And old Bottleby's hearty guffaws
As he drove at my ribs with his knuckles,

His mode of expressing applause:
While Jean Bottleby—queenly Miss Janet—
Drew her handkerchief hastily out,
In fits at my slyness—what can it
Have all been about?

I know 'twas the happiest, quaintest
Combination of pathos and fun:
But I've got no idea—the faintest—
Of what was the actual pun.
I think it was somehow connected
With something I'd recently read—
Or heard—or perhaps recollected
On going to bed.

What had I been reading? The *Standard*:
"Double Bigamy"; "Speech of the Mayor."
And later—eh? yes! I meandered
Through some chapters of "Vanity Fair."
How it fuses the grave with the festive!
Yet e'en there, there is nothing so fine—
So playfully, subtly suggestive—
As that joke of mine.

Did it hinge upon "parting asunder?"
No, I don't part my hair with my brush.
Was the point of it "hair"? Now I wonder!
Stop a bit—I shall think of it—hush!
There's hare, a wild animal—stuff!
It was something a deal more recondite:
Of that I am certain enough;

And of nothing beyond it.

Hair—locks! There are probably many
Good things to be said about those.
Give me time—that's the best guess of any—
"Lock" has several meanings, one knows.
Iron locks—iron-gray-locks—a "deadlock"—
That would set up an everyday wit:
Then of course there's the obvious "wedlock";
But that wasn't it.

No! mine was a joke for the ages;
Full of intricate meaning and pith;
A feast for your scholars and sages—
How it would have rejoiced Sydney Smith!
'Tis such thoughts that ennoble a mortal;
And, singling him out from the herd,
Fling wide immortality's portal—
But what was the word?

Ah me! 'tis a bootless endeavor.
As the flight of a bird of the air
Is the flight of a joke—you will never
See the same one again, you may swear.
'Twas my firstborn, and O how I prized it!
My darling, my treasure, my own!
This brain and none other devised it—
And now it has flown.

Charles Stuart Calverley.

LOVE

CANST thou love me, lady?
I've not learn'd to woo;
Thou art on the shady
Side of sixty, too.
Still I love thee dearly!
Thou hast lands and pelf:
But I love thee merely
Merely for thyself.

Wilt thou love me, fairest?
Though thou art not fair;
And I think thou wearest
Someone-else's hair.
Thou could'st love, though, dearly;
And, as I am told,
Thou art very nearly
Worth thy weight in gold.

Dost thou love me, sweet one?
Tell me that thou dost!
Women fairly beat one,
But I think thou must.
Thou art loved so dearly:
I am plain, but then
Thou (to speak sincerely)
Art as plain again.

Love me, bashful fairy!
I've an empty purse:
And I've "moods," which vary;

Mostly for the worst.
Still, I love thee dearly:
Though I make (I feel)
Love a little queerly,
I'm as true as steel.

Love me, swear to love me
(As you know, they do)
By yon heaven above me
And its changeless blue.
Love me, lady, dearly,
If you'll be so good;
Though I don't see clearly
On what ground you should.

Love me—ah! or love me
Not, but be my bride!
Do not simply shove me
(So to speak) aside!
P'raps it would be dearly
Purchased at the price;
But a hundred yearly
Would be very nice.

Charles Stuart Calverley.

SINCE WE PARTED

SINCE we parted yester eve,
I do love thee, love, believe,
Twelve times dearer, twelve hours longer,
One dream deeper, one night stronger,
One sun surer,—thus much more
Than I loved thee, love, before.

Owen Meredith.

A KISS—BY MISTAKE

UPON the railway train we met—
She had the softest, bluest eyes,
A face you never could forget—
"Sixteen" with all that that implies.
I knew her once a little girl,
And meeting now a mutual friend,
Our thoughts and hearts got in a whirl;
We talked for miles without much end,

I threw my arms around the seat
Where, just in front, she sideways sat,
Her melting eyes and face to meet—
(And no one wondered much at that),
For soon the station where she left
Would on the sorrowing vision rise,
And I at least should feel bereft;
I thought a tear stood in her eyes.

She was but kith, not kin of mine;
Ten years had passed since last we met,
And when in going she did incline
Her face 'twas natural to forget,
It seemed so like a child I knew—
I met her half way by mistake;
And coming near those eyes of blue,
She gently kissed me—by mistake!

She saw her error, and straightway ran
With flaming blushes, rosy red;
I should not be one-half a man

If thoughts of wrong came in my head;
In fact, I'd take that very train
And travel daily for her sake,
If she would only come again
And gently kiss me—by mistake!

Joel Benton.

A GAME OF FIVES

FIVE little girls, of Five, Four, Three, Two, One:
Rolling on the hearthrug, full of tricks and fun.

Five rosy girls, in years from Ten to Six:
Sitting down to lessons—no more time for tricks.

Five growing girls, from Fifteen to Eleven:
Music, Drawing, Languages, and food enough for seven!

Five winsome girls, from Twenty to Sixteen:
Each young man that calls, I say "Now tell me which you *mean!*"

Five dashing girls, the youngest Twenty-one:
But, if nobody proposes, what is there to be done?

Five showy girls—but Thirty is an age
When girls may be engaging, but they somehow don't engage.

Five dressy girls, of Thirty-one or more:
So gracious to the shy young men they snubbed so much before!

Five *passé* girls—Their age? Well, never mind!
We jog along together, like the rest of human kind:
But the quondam "careless bachelor" begins to think he knows
The answer to that ancient problem "how the money goes!"

Lewis Carroll.

A VALENTINE

(Sent to a friend who complained that I was glad enough to see him when he came, but didn't seem to miss him if he stayed away.)

AND cannot pleasures, while they last,
Be actual unless, when past,
They leave us shuddering and aghast,
With anguish smarting?
And cannot friends be firm and fast,
And yet bear parting?

And must I then, at Friendship's call,
Calmly resign the little all
(Trifling, I grant, it is and small)
I have of gladness,
And lend my being to the thrall
Of gloom and sadness?

And think you that I should be dumb,
And full *dolorum omnium*,
Excepting when you choose to come
And share my dinner?
At other times be sour and glum
And daily thinner?

Must he then only live to weep,
Who'd prove his friendship true and deep?
By day a lonely shadow creep,
At night-time languish,
Oft raising in his broken sleep
The moan of anguish.

The lover, if for certain days
His fair one be denied his gaze,
Sinks not in grief and wild amaze,
But, wiser wooer
He spends the time in writing lays,
And posts them to her.

And if the verse flow free and fast,
Till even the poet is aghast,
A touching Valentine at last
The post shall carry,
When thirteen days are gone and past
Of February.

Farewell, dear friend, and when we meet,
In desert waste or crowded street,
Perhaps before this week shall fleet,
Perhaps to-morrow,
I trust to find your heart the seat
Of wasting sorrow.

Lewis Carroll.

THE WEDDING DAY

I

SWEETHEART, name the day for me
When we two shall wedded be.
Make it ere another moon,
While the meadows are in tune,
And the trees are blossoming,
And the robins mate and sing.
Whisper, love, and name a day
In this merry month of May.

No, no, no,
You shall not escape me so!
Love will not forever wait;
Roses fade when gathered late.

II

Fie, for shame, Sir Malcontent!
How can time be better spent
Than in wooing? I would wed
When the clover blossoms red,
When the air is full of bliss,
And the sunshine like a kiss.
If you're good I'll grant a boon:
You shall have me, sir, in June.

Nay, nay, nay,
Girls for once should have their way!
If you love me, wait till June:
Rosebuds wither, picked too soon.

Edmund Clarence Stedman.

EDGED TOOLS

WELL, Helen, quite two years have flown
Since that enchanted, dreamy night,
When you and I were left alone,
And wondered whether they were right
Who said that each the other loved;
And thus debating, yes and no,
And half in earnest, as it proved,
We bargained to pretend 'twas so.

Two sceptic children of the world,
Each with a heart engraven o'er
With broken love-knots, quaintly curled,
Of hot flirtations held before;
Yet, somehow, either seemed to find,
This time, a something more akin
To that young, natural love,—the kind
Which comes but once, and breaks us in.

What sweetly stolen hours we knew,
And frolics perilous as gay!
Though lit in sport, Love's taper grew
More bright and burning day by day.
We knew each heart was only lent,
The other's ancient scars to heal:
The very thought a pathos blent
With all the mirth we tried to feel.

How bravely when the time to part
Came with the wanton season's close,
Though nature with our mutual art

Had mingled more than either chose,
We smothered Love, upon the verge
Of folly, in one last embrace,
And buried him without a dirge,
And turned, and left his resting-place.

Yet often (tell me what it means!)
His spirit steals upon me here,
Far, far away from all the scenes
His little lifetime held so dear;
He comes: I hear a mystic strain
In which some tender memory lies;
I dally with your hair again;
I catch the gleam of violet eyes.

Ah, Helen! how have matters been
Since those rude obsequies, with you?
Say, is my partner in the sin
A sharer of the penance too?
Again the vision's at my side:
I drop my head upon my breast,
And wonder if he really died,
And why his spirit will not rest.

Edmund Clarence Stedman.

WITCHCRAFT

OUR great-great-grandpapas had schooled
Your fancies, Lita, were you born
In days when Cotton Mather ruled
And damask petticoats were worn!
Your pretty ways, your mocking air,
Had passed, mayhap, for Satan's wiles—
As fraught with danger, then and there,
To you, as now to us your smiles.

Why not? Were inquest to begin,
The tokens are not far to seek:
Item—the dimple of your chin;
Item—that freckle on your cheek.
Grace shield his simple soul from harm
Who enters yon flirtation niche,
Or trusts in whispered counter-charm,
Alone with such a parlous witch!

Your fan a wand is, in disguise;
It conjures, and we straight are drawn
Within a witches' Paradise
Of music, germans, roses, lawn.
So through the season, where you go,
All else than Lita men forget:
One needs no second-sight to know
That sorcery is rampant yet.

Now, since the bars no more await
Fair maids that practise sable arts,
Take heed, while I pronounce the fate

Of her who thus ensnares men's hearts:
In time you shall a wizard meet
With spells more potent than your own,
And you shall know your master, Sweet,
And for these witcheries atone.

For you at his behest shall wear
A veil, and seek with him the church,
And at the altar rail forswear
The craft that left you in the lurch;
But oft thereafter, musing long,
With smile and sigh, and conscience-twitch,
You shall too late confess the wrong—
A captive and repentant witch.

Edmund Clarence Stedman.

TOUJOURS AMOUR

PRITHEE tell me, Dimple-Chin,
At what age doth love begin?
Your blue eyes have scarcely seen
Summers three, my fairy queen,
But a miracle of sweets,
Soft approaches, sly retreats,
Show the little archer there,
Hidden in your pretty hair;
When didst learn a heart to win?
Prithee tell me, Dimple-Chin!

"Oh!" the rosy lips reply,
"I can't tell you if I try.
'Tis so long I can't remember:
Ask some younger lass than I!"

Tell, O tell me, Grizzled-Face,
Do your heart and head keep pace?
When does hoary Love expire,
When do frosts put out the fire?
Can its embers burn below
All that chill December snow?
Care you still soft hands to press,
Bonny heads to smooth and bless?
When does Love give up the chase?
Tell, O tell me, Grizzled-Face?

"Ah!" the wise old lips reply,
"Youth may pass, and strength may die;
But of Love I can't foretoken:

Ask some older sage than I!"

Edmund Clarence Stedman.

DICTUM SAPIENTI

THAT 'tis well to be off with the old love
Before one is on with the new
Has somehow passed into a proverb,—
But I never have found it true.

No love can be quite like the old love,
Whate'er may be said for the new—
And if you dismiss me, my darling,
You may come to this thinking, too.

Were the proverb not wiser if mended,
And the fickle and wavering told
To be sure they're on with the new love
Before they are off with the old?

Charles Henry Webb.

UNDOWERED

THOU hast not gold? Why, this is gold
All clustering round thy forehead white;
And were it weighed, and were it told,
I could not say its worth to-night!

Thou hast not wit? Why, what is this
Wherewith thou capturest many a wight,
Who doth forget a tongue is his,
As I well-nigh forgot to-night?

Nor station? Well, ah, well! I own
Thou hast no place assured thee quite;
So now I raise thee to a throne;
Begin thy reign, my Queen, to-night.

Harriet McEwen Kimball.

THE LOVE-KNOT

TYING her bonnet under her chin,
She tied her raven ringlets in;
But not alone in the silken snare
Did she catch her lovely floating hair,
For tying her bonnet under her chin,
She tied a young man's heart within.

They were strolling together up the hill,
Where the wind comes blowing merry and chill;
And it blew the curls, a frolicsome race,
All over the happy peach-colored face,
Till, scolding and laughing, she tied them in,
Under her beautiful dimpled chin.

And it blew a color, bright as the bloom
Of the pinkest fuchsia's tossing plume,
All over the cheeks of the prettiest girl
That ever imprisoned a romping curl,
Or, tying her bonnet under her chin,
Tied a young man's heart within.

Steeper and steeper grew the hill;
Madder, merrier, chillier still
The western wind blew down and played
The wildest tricks with the little maid,
As, tying her bonnet under her chin,
She tied a young man's heart within.

O western wind, do you think it was fair
To play such tricks with her floating hair?

To gladly, gleefully do your best
To blow her against the young man's breast,
Where he as gladly folded her in,
And kissed her mouth and her dimpled chin?

Ah! Ellery Vane, you little thought,
An hour ago, when you besought
This country lass to walk with you,
After the sun had dried the dew,
What perilous danger you'd be in,
As she tied her bonnet under her chin

Nora Perry.

VERS DE SOCIÉTÉ

THERE, pay it, James! 'tis cheaply earned;
My conscience! how one's cabman charges!
But never mind, so I'm returned
Safe to my native street of Clarges.
I've just an hour for one cigar
(What style these Reinas have, and what ash!)
One hour to watch the evening star
With just one Curaçoa-and-potash.

Ah me! that face beneath the leaves
And blossoms of its piquant bonnet!
Who would have thought that forty thieves
Of years had laid their fingers on it!
Could you have managed to enchant
At Lord's to-day old lovers simple,
Had Robber Time not played gallant,
And spared you every youthful dimple!

That Robber bold, like courtier Claude,
Who danced the gay coranto jesting,
By your bright beauty charmed and awed,
Has bowed and passed you unmolesting.
No feet of many-wintered crows
Have traced about your eyes a wrinkle;
Your sunny hair has thawed the snows
That other heads with silver sprinkle.

I wonder if that pair of gloves
I won of you you'll ever pay me!
I wonder if our early loves

Were wise or foolish, Cousin Amy?
I wonder if our childish tiff
Now seems to you, like me, a blunder!
I wonder if you wonder if
I ever wonder if you wonder.

I wonder if you'd think it bliss
Once more to be the fashion's leader!
I wonder if the trick of this
Escapes the unsuspecting reader!
And as for him who does or can
Delight in it, I wonder whether
He knows that almost any man
Could reel it off by yards together!

I wonder if—What's that? A knock?
Is that you, James? Eh? What? God bless me!
How time has flown! It's eight o'clock,
And here's my fellow come to dress me.
Be quick, or I shall be the guest
Whom Lady Mary never pardons;
I trust you, James, to do your best
To save the soup at Grosvenor Gardens.

H. D. Traill.

A LETTER OF ADVICE

WHEN you love—as all men will—
Sing the theme of your devotion,
Sue—and vow—and worship still—
Overflow with deep emotion,
Bow to Cupid's sweet decrees,
Lightly wear the happy fetter,
Bend the knee and plead! But please,
Do not write your love a letter!

Ah! most tempting it may be:
Ink flows free—and pens will write,
And your passion fain you'd see
Plainly mapped in black and white.
Yet refrain from shedding ink,
If you can:—'tis wiser—better.
Ere you pen a sentence, think!
Do not write your love a letter.

Hearts may cool, and views may change—
Other scenes may seem inviting,
But a heart can't safely range
If committed 'tis to writing.
What you've written is a writ,
Holds you closely as a debtor.
Will she spare you? Not a bit!
Do not write your love a letter!

Think of Breach of Promise cause,
Think of barristers provoking,
Leading you to slips and flaws,

Turning all your love to joking.
If you've written aught, they'll be
Safe to find it as a setter—
Then you'll wish you'd hearkened me—
Do not write your love a letter!

Oh, those letters read in Court!
How the tender things seem stupid!
How deep feeling seems but sport!
How young Momus trips up Cupid!
Take my warning then—or soon,
O'er your folly you'll be fretter,
Saying, "Why, poor, foolish spoon,
Did I write my love a letter?"

Thomas Hood, Jr.

AT THE LATTICE

BEHIND the curtain,

With glance uncertain,

Peeps pet Florence as I gaily ride;

Half demurely,

But, though purely

Most, most surely

Wishing she were riding, riding by my side.

In leafy alleys,

Where sunlight dallies,

Pleasant were it, bonnie, to be riding rein by rein;

And where summer tosses,

All about in bosses,

Velvet verdant mosses,

Still more pleasant, surely, to dismount again.

O thou Beauty!

Hanging ripe and fruity

At the muslined lattice in the drooping eve,

Whisper from the casement

If that blushing face meant,

"At the cottage basement,

Gallant, halt, I come to thee; I come to never leave."

But if those coy lashes

Stir for whoso dashes

Past the scented window in the fading light,

Close the lattice, sweetest;

Darkness were discreetest;

And, with bridle fleetest,

I will gallop onwards, unattended through the night.

Alfred Austin.

FRENCH WITH A MASTER

TEACH you French? I will, my dear!
Sit and con your lesson here.
What did Adam say to Eve?
Aimer, aimer; c'est à vivre.

Don't pronounce the last word long;
Make it short to suit the song;
Rhyme it to your flowing sleeve,
Aimer, aimer; c'est à vivre.

Sleeve, I said, but what's the harm
If I really meant your arm?
Mine shall twine it (by your leave),
Aimer, aimer; c'est à vivre.

Learning French is full of slips;
Do as I do with the lips;
Here's the right way, you perceive,
Aimer, aimer; c'est à vivre.

French is always spoken best
Breathing deeply from the chest;
Darling, does your bosom heave?
Aimer, aimer; c'est à vivre.

Now, my dainty little sprite,
Have I taught your lesson right?
Then what pay shall I receive?
Aimer, aimer; c'est à vivre.

Will you think me overbold
If I linger to be told

Whether you yourself believe
Aimer, aimer; c'est à vivre.

Pretty pupil, when you say
All this French to me to-day,
Do you mean it, or deceive?
Aimer, aimer; c'est à vivre.

Tell me, may I understand,
When I press your little hand,
That our hearts together cleave?
Aimer, aimer; c'est à vivre.

Have you in your tresses room
For some orange-buds to bloom?
May I such a garland weave?
Aimer, aimer; c'est à vivre.

Or, if I presume too much
Teaching French by sense of touch,
Grant me pardon and reprieve!
Aimer, aimer; c'est à vivre.

Sweetheart, no! you cannot go!
Let me sit and hold you so;
Adam did the same to Eve,—
Aimer, aimer; c'est à vivre.

Theodore Tilton.

ON AN INTAGLIO HEAD OF MINERVA

THE cunning hand that carved this face,
A little helmeted Minerva—
The hand, I say, ere Phidias wrought,
Had lost its subtle skill and fervour.

Who was he? Was he glad or sad?
Who knew to carve in such a fashion?
Perchance he shaped this dainty head
For some brown girl that Scorned his passion.

But he is dust: we may not know
His happy or unhappy story:
Nameless and dead these thousand years,
His work outlives him—there's his glory!

Both man and jewel lay in earth
Beneath a lava-buried city;
The thousand summers came and went,
With neither haste, nor hate, nor pity.

The years wiped out the man, but left
The jewel fresh as any blossom.
Till some Visconti dug it up,
To rise and fall on Mabel's bosom.

O Roman brother! see how Time
Your gracious handiwork has guarded;
See how your loving, patient art
Has come, at last, to be rewarded.

Who would not suffer slights of men
And pangs of hopeless passion also,

To have his carven agate-stone
On such a bosom rise and fall so!

Thomas Bailey Aldrich.

THE LUNCH

A GOTHIC window, where a damask curtain
Made the blank daylight shadowy and uncertain:
A slab of agate ore four Eagle-talons
Held trimly up and neatly taught to balance:
A porcelain dish, o'er which in many a cluster
Black grapes hung down, dead ripe and without lustre:
A melon cut in thin, delicious slices:
A cake that seemed mosaic-work in spices:
Two China cups with golden tulips sunny,
And rich inside with chocolate like honey:
And she and I the banquet-scene completing
With dreamy words—and very pleasant eating.

Thomas Bailey Aldrich.

THE WITCH IN THE GLASS

"MY mother says I must not pass
Too near that glass;
She is afraid that I will see
A little witch that looks like me,
With a red, red mouth to whisper low
The very thing I should not know!"

"Alack for all your mother's care!
A bird of the air,
A wistful wind, or (I suppose)
Sent by some hapless boy—a rose,
With breath too sweet, will whisper low
The very thing you should not know!"

Sarah Morgan Bryan Piatt.

TO PHŒBE

"GENTLE, modest, little flower,
Sweet epitome of May,
Love me but for half-an-hour,
Love me, love me, little Fay."
Sentences so fiercely flaming
In your tiny shell-like ear,
I should always be exclaiming,
If I loved you, Phœbe, dear!

"Smiles that thrill from any distance
Shed upon me while I sing!
Please ecstaticise existence;
Love me, oh, thou fairy thing!"
Words like these, outpouring sadly,
You'd perpetually hear,
If I loved you, fondly, madly;—
But I do not, Phœbe, dear!

William Schwenck Gilbert.

MY LOVE AND MY HEART

OH, the days were ever shiny
When I ran to meet my love;
When I press'd her hand so tiny
Through her tiny tiny glove.
Was I very deeply smitten?
Oh, I loved like anything!
But my love she is a kitten,
And my heart's a ball of string.

She was pleasingly poetic,
And she loved my little rhymes;
For our tastes were sympathetic,
In the old and happy times.
Oh, the ballads I have written,
And have taught my love to sing!
But my love she is a kitten,
And my heart's a ball of string.

Would she listen to my offer,
On my knees I would impart
A sincere and ready proffer
Of my hand and of my heart.
And below her dainty mitten
I would fix a wedding ring—
But my love she is a kitten,
And my heart's a ball of string.

Take a warning, happy lover,
From the moral that I show;
Or too late you may discover

What I learn'd a month ago.

We are scratch'd or we are bitten

By the pets to whom we cling.

Oh, my love she is a kitten,

And my heart's a ball of string.

Henry S. Leigh.

TO A COUNTRY COUSIN

CRUEL Cousin Kate, you ask me
For a lyric or a lay.
How tyrannical to task me,
Cousin Kate, in such a way.
Pardon me, I pray, and pity—
(Oh, do anything but frown!)
For I can't be wise or witty
In an album out of town

No, my Pegasus will canter
Only here on civic stones;
In the country I instanter
Come to grief and broken bones.
Be it mine to sing the city,
Where I seek my mild renown;—
But I can't be wise or witty
In an album out of town.

Small my power and small my will is
Rural sympathies to win;
Ludgate my sublimest hill is,
And my fields are Lincoln's Inn
All the Muses in committee,
Pouring inspiration down,
Cannot make me wise or witty
In an album out of town.

London life in many phases
I describe for Cockney friends;
Lead me out among the daisies

And my versifying ends.
I can favor with a ditty
Jones, and Robinson, and Brown;
But I can't be wise or witty
In an album out of town.

Cousin, hear my supplication;
Give me something else to do.
Is there aught in all creation
I would not attempt for you?
Ask my life, my cruel Kitty:
Bid me hang, or bid me drown;
But I can't be wise or witty
In an album out of town.

Henry S. Leigh.

THE FAMILY FOOL

OH! a private buffoon is a light-hearted loon,
If you listen to popular rumour;
From morning to night he's so joyous and bright,
And he bubbles with wit and good humour!
He's so quaint and so terse, both in prose and in verse;
Yet though people forgive his transgression,
There are one or two rules that all Family Fools
Must observe if they love their profession.
There are one or two rules,
Half-a-dozen, maybe,
That all family fools,
Of whatever degree,
Must observe, if they love their profession.

If you wish to succeed as a jester, you'll need
To consider each person's auricular:
What is all right for B. would quite scandalize C.
(For C. is so very particular);
And D. may be dull, and E.'s very thick skull
Is as empty of brains as a ladle;
While F. is F sharp, and will cry with a carp,
That he's known your best joke from his cradle!
When your humour they flout,
You can't let yourself go;
And it *does* put you out
When a person says, "Oh!
I have known that old joke from my cradle!"

If your master is surly, from getting up early

(And tempers are short in the morning),
An inopportune joke is enough to provoke
Him to give you, at once, a month's warning.
Then if you refrain, he is at you again,
For he likes to get value for money,
He'll ask then and there, with an insolent stare,
"If you know that you're paid to be funny?"
It adds to the tasks
Of a merryman's place,
When your principal asks,
With a scowl on his face,
If you know that you're paid to be funny?

Comes a Bishop, maybe, or a solemn D.D.—
Oh! beware of his anger provoking
Better not pull his hair—don't stick pins in his chair;
He won't understand practical joking.
If the jests that you crack have an orthodox smack,
You may get a bland smile from these sages;
But should it, by chance, be imported from France,
Half-a-crown is stopped out of your wages!
It's a general rule,
Though your zeal it may quench
If the Family Fool
Makes a joke that's too French,
Half-a-crown is stopped out of his wages!

Though your head it may rack with a bilious attack,
And your senses with toothache you're losing,
Don't be mopy and flat—they don't fine you for that
If you're properly quaint and amusing!

Though your wife ran away with a soldier that day
And took with her your trifle of money;
Bless your heart, they don't mind—they're exceedingly kind—
They don't blame you—as long as you're funny!
It's a comfort to feel
If your partner should flit,
Though you suffer a deal,
They don't mind it a bit—
They don't blame you—so long as you're funny!

W. S. Gilbert.

AN INTERLUDE

IN the greenest growth of the May-time,
I rode where the woods were wet,
Between the dawn and the day-time;
The spring was glad that we met.

There was something the season wanted,
Though the ways and the woods smelt sweet;
The breath at your lips that panted,
The pulse of the grass at your feet.

You came, and the sun came after,
And the green grew golden above;
And the May-flowers lightened with laughter,
And the meadow-sweet shook with love.

Your feet in the full-grown grasses
Moved soft as a weak wind blows;
You passed me as April passes,
With face made out of a rose.

By the stream where the stems were slender,
Your light foot paused at the sedge;
It might be to watch the tender
Light leaves in the spring-time hedge.

On boughs that the sweet month blanches
With flowery frost of May;
It might be a bird in the branches,
It might be a thorn in the way.

I waited to watch you linger,
With foot drawn back from the dew,

Till a sunbeam straight like a finger
Struck sharp through the leaves at you.

And a bird overhead sang "Follow,"
And a bird to the right sang "Here";
And the arch of the leaves was hollow,
And the meaning of May was clear.

I saw where the sun's hand pointed,
I knew what the bird's note said;
By the dawn and the dew fall anointed,
You were queen by the gold on your head.

As the glimpse of a burnt-out ember
Recalls a regret of the sun,
I remember, forget, and remember
What love saw done and undone.

I remember the way we parted,
The day and the way we met;
You hoped we were both broken-hearted,
And knew we should both forget.

And May with her world in flower
Seemed still to murmur and smile
As you murmured and smiled for an hour;
I saw you twice at the stile.

A hand like a white-wood blossom
You lifted and waved, and passed,
With head hung down to the bosom,
And pale, as it seemed, to the last.

And the best and the worst of this is,

That neither is most to blame,
If you've forgotten my kisses,
And I've forgotten your name.

Algernon Charles Swinburne.

A MATCH

IF love were what the rose is,
And I were like the leaf,
Our lives would grow together
In sad or singing weather,
Blown fields or flowerful closes,
Green pleasure or grey grief;
If love were what the rose is,
And I were like the leaf.

If I were what the words are,
And love were like the tune,
With double sound and single
Delight our lips would mingle,
With kisses glad as birds are
That get sweet rain at noon;
If I were what the words are,
And love were like the tune.

If you were Life, my darling,
And I, your love, were Death,
We'd shine and snow together
Ere March made sweet the wreath
With daffodil and starling
And hours of fruitful breath;
If you were Life, my darling,
And I, your love, were Death.

If you were thrall to Sorrow,
And I were page to Joy,
We'd play for lives and seasons

With loving looks and treasons,
And tears of night and morrow,
And laughs of maid and boy;
If you were thrall to Sorrow,
And I were page to Joy.

If you were April's lady,
And I were lord in May,
We'd throw with leaves for hours,
And draw for days with flowers,
Till day like night were shady,
And night were bright like day;
If you were April's lady,
And I were lord in May.

If you were queen of pleasure
And I were king of pain,
We'd hunt down Love together,
Pluck out his flying feather,
And teach his feet a measure,
And find his mouth a rein;
If you were queen of pleasure,
And I were king of pain.

Algernon Charles Swinburne.

CAPRICE

I

SHE hung the cage at the window:
"If he goes by," she said,
"He will hear my robin singing,
And when he lifts his head,
I shall be sitting here to sew,
And he will bow to me, I know."

The robin sang a love-sweet song,
The young man raised his head;
The maiden turned away and blushed:
"I am a fool!" she said,
And went on 'broidering in silk
A pink-eyed rabbit, white as milk.

II

The young man loitered slowly
By the house three times that day;
She took her bird from the window:
"He need not look this way."
She sat at her piano long,
And sighed, and played a death-sad song.

But when the day was done, she said,
"I wish that he would come!
Remember, Mary, if he calls
To-night—I'm not at home."
So when he rang, she went—the elf!—
She went and let him in herself.

III

They sang full long together
Their songs love-sweet, death-sad;
The robin woke from his slumber,
And rang out, clear and glad.
"Now go!" she coldly said; "'tis late";
And followed him—to latch the gate.

He took the rosebud from her hair,
While, "You shall not!" she said;
He closed her hand within his own,
And, while her tongue forbade,
Her will was darkened in the eclipse
Of blinding love upon his lips.

William Dean Howells.

THE MINUET

GRANDMA told me all about it,
Told me so I couldn't doubt it,
How she danced—my Grandma danced!—
Long ago.
How she held her pretty head,
How her dainty skirt she spread,
Turning out her little toes;
How she slowly leaned and rose—
Long ago.

Grandma's hair was bright and sunny;
Dimpled cheeks, too—ah, how funny!
Really quite a pretty girl,
Long ago.
Bless her! why she wears a cap,
Grandma does, and takes a nap
Every single day; and yet
Grandma danced the minuet
Long ago.

Now she sits there rocking, rocking,
Always knitting Grandpa's stocking—
(Every girl was taught to knit
Long ago),
Yet her figure is so neat,
And her ways so staid and sweet,
I can almost see her now
Bending to her partner's bow,
Long ago.

Grandma says our modern jumping,
Hopping, rushing, whirling, bumping,
Would have shocked the gentle folk
Long ago.
No—they moved with stately grace,
Everything in proper place,
Gliding slowly forward, then
Slowly curtseying back again.
Long ago.

Modern ways are quite alarming,
Grandma says; but boys were charming—
Girls and boys I mean, of course—
Long ago.
Bravely modest, grandly shy,—
She would like to have us try
Just to feel like those who met
In the graceful minuet
Long ago.

With the minuet in fashion,
Who could fly into a passion?
All would wear the calm they wore
Long ago.
In time to come, if I, perchance,
Should tell my grandchild of our dance,
I should really like to say,
"We did it, dear, in some such way,
Long ago."

Mary Mapes Dodge.

A STREET SKETCH

UPON the Kerb, a maiden neat—
Her hazel eyes are passing sweet—
There stands and waits in dire distress:
The muddy road is pitiless,
And 'busses thunder down the street!

A snowy skirt, all frills and pleat;
Two tiny, well-shod, dainty feet
Peep out, beneath her kilted dress,
Upon the Kerb.

She'll first advance, and then retreat,
Half-frightened by a hansom fleet.
She looks around, I must confess,
With marvellous coquettishness!—
Then droops her eyes and looks discreet,
Upon the Kerb!

J. Ashby-Sterry.

SAINT MAY
A CITY LYRIC

ST. ALOYS THE GREAT is both mouldy and grim,
Not knowing the road there, you'll long have to search
To find your way into this old city church;
Yet on fine Sunday mornings I frequently stray
There to see a new saint, whom I've christened St. May.

Of saints I've seen plenty in churches before—
In Florence or Venice they're there by the score;
Agnese, Maria—the rest I forget—
By Titian, Bassano, and brave Tintoret:
They none can compare, though they're well in their way,
In maidenly grace with my dainty St. May.

She's young for a saint, for she's scarcely eighteen,
And ne'er could wear peas in those dainty *bottines;*
Her locks are not shaven, and 'twould be a sin
To wear a hair-shirt next that delicate skin;
Save diagonal stripes on a dress of light gray,
Stripes ne'er have been borne by bewitching St. May.

Then she's almost too plump and too round for a saint,
With sweet little dimples that Millais might paint;
She has no mediæval nor mortified mien,
No wimple of yellow, nor background of green,
A nimbus of hair throws its sunshiny ray
Of glory around the fair face of St. May.

What surquayne or partlet could look better than
My saint's curly jacket of black Astracan?
What coif than her bonnet—a triumph of skill—

Or alb than her petticoat edged with a frill?
So sober, yet smiling—so grave, yet so gay,
Oh, where is a saint like my charming St. May?

J. Ashby-Sterry.

PET'S PUNISHMENT

OH, if my love offended me,
And we had words together,
To show her I would master be,
I'd whip her with a feather!

If then she, like a naughty girl,
Would tyranny declare it,
I'd give my pet a cross of pearl,
And make her always bear it.

If still she tried to sulk and sigh,
And threw away my posies,
I'd catch my darling on the sly,
And smother her with roses!

But should she clench her dimpled fists,
Or contradict her betters,
I'd manacle her tiny wrists
With dainty golden fetters.

And if she dared her lips to pout—
Like many pert young misses—
I'd wind my arm her waist about,
And punish her—with kisses!

J. Ashby-Sterry.

HER LETTER

I'M sitting alone by the fire,
Dressed just as I came from the dance,
In a robe even *you* would admire—
It cost a cool thousand in France;
I'm be-diamonded out of all reason,
My hair is done up in a queue:
In short, sir, "the belle of the season"
Is wasting an hour on you.

A dozen engagements I've broken;
I left in the midst of a set;
Likewise a proposal, half spoken,
That waits—on the stairs—for me yet.
They say he'll be rich—when he grows up—
And then he adores me indeed.
And you, sir, are turning your nose up,
Three thousand miles off, as you read.

"And how do I like my position?"
"And what do I think of New York?"
"And now, in my higher ambition,
With whom do I waltz, flirt, or talk?"
"And isn't it nice to have riches,
And diamonds and silks, and all that?"
"And isn't it a change to the ditches
And tunnels of Poverty Flat?"

Well, yes—if you saw us out driving
Each day in the Park, four-in-hand—
If you saw poor dear mamma contriving

To look supernaturally grand—
If you saw papa's picture, as taken
By Brady, and tinted at that—
You'd never suspect he sold bacon
And flour at Poverty Flat.

And yet, just this moment when sitting
In the glare of the grand chandelier—
In the bustle and glitter befitting
The "finest *soirée* of the year"—
In the mists of a *gaze de Chambéry*,
And the hum of the smallest of talk—
Somehow, Joe, I thought of the "Ferry,"
And the dance that we had on "The Fork";

Of Harrison's barn, with its muster
Of flags festooned over the wall;
Of the candles that shed their soft lustre
And tallow on head-dress and shawl;
Of the steps that we took to one fiddle;
Of the dress of my queer *vis-a-vis*,
And how I once went down the middle
With the man that shot Sandy McGee;

Of the moon that was quietly sleeping
On the hill, when the time came to go;
Of the few baby peaks that were peeping
From under their bedclothes of snow;
Of that ride—that to me was the rarest;
Of—the something you said at the gate.
Ah, Joe, then I wasn't an heiress

To "the best-paying lead in the State!"

Well, well, it's all past; yet it's funny
To think, as I stood in the glare
Of fashion and beauty and money,
That I should be thinking, right there,
Of some one who breasted high water,
And swam the North Fork, and all that,
Just to dance with old Folinsbee's daughter,
The Lily of Poverty Flat.

But goodness! what nonsense I'm writing!
(Mama says my taste still is low),
Instead of my triumphs reciting,
I'm spooning on Joseph—heigh-ho!
And I'm to be "finished" by travel—
Whatever's the meaning of that—
Oh! why did papa strike pay gravel
In drifting on Poverty Flat?

Good-night—here's the end of my paper;
Good-night—if the longitude please—
For maybe, while wasting my taper,
Your sun's climbing over the trees.
But know, if you haven't got riches,
And are poor, dearest Joe, and all that,
That my heart's somewhere there in the ditches,
And you've struck it—on Poverty Flat.

Francis Bret Harte.

AVICE

THOUGH the voice of modern schools
Has demurred,
By the dreamy Asian creed
'Tis averred,
That the souls of men, released
From their bodies when deceased,
Sometimes enter in a beast,—
Or a bird.

I have watched you long, Avice,—
Watched you so,
I have found your secret out;
And I know
That the restless ribboned things,
Where your slope of shoulder springs,
Are but undeveloped wings,
That will grow.

When you enter in a room,
It is stirred
With the wayward, flashing flight
Of a bird;
And you speak—and bring with your
Leaf and sun-ray, bud and blue,
And the wind-breath and the dew,
At a word.

When you called to me my name,
Then again
When I heard your single cry

In the lane,
All the sound was as the "sweet"
Which the birds to birds repeat
In their thank-song to the heat
After rain.

When you sang the Schwalbenlied,—
'Twas absurd,—
But it seemed no human note
That I heard;
For your strain had all the trills,
All the little shakes and stills,
Of the over-song that rills
From a bird.

You have just their eager, quick
Airs *de tête*,
All their flush and fever-heat
When elate;
Every bird-like nod and beck,
And a bird's own curve of neck
When she gives a little peck
To her mate.

When you left me, only now,
In that furred,
Puffed, and feathered Polish dress,
I was spurred
Just to catch you, O my sweet,
By the bodice trim and neat,—
Just to feel your heart-a-beat,

Like a bird.

Yet alas! Love's light you deign
But to wear
As the dew upon your plumes,
And you care
Not a whit for rest or hush;
But the leaves, the lyric gush,
And the wing-power, and the rush
Of the air.

So I dare not woo you, sweet,
For a day,
Lest I lose you in a flash,
As I may;
Did I tell you tender things,
You would shake your sudden wings;—
You would start from him who sings,
And away.

Austin Dobson.

A SONG OF THE FOUR SEASONS

WHEN Spring comes laughing
By vale and hill,
By wind-flower walking
And daffodil,—
Sing stars of morning,
Sing morning skies,
Sing blue of Speedwell,—
And my Love's eyes.

When comes the Summer,
Full-leaved and strong,
And gay birds gossip
The orchard long,—
Sing hid, sweet honey
That no bee sips;
Sing red, red roses,—
And my love's lips.

When Autumn scatters
The leaves again,
And piled sheaves bury
The broad-wheeled wain,—
Sing flutes of harvest
Where men rejoice;
Sing rounds of reapers,—
And my Love's voice.

But when comes winter
With hail and storm,
And red fire roaring

And ingle warm,—
Sing first sad going
Of friends that part;
Then sing glad meeting,—
And my Love's heart.

Austin Dobson.

IN TOWN

"The blue fly sung in the pane."—TENNYSON.

TOILING in Town now is "horrid"
(There is that woman again!)—
June in the zenith is torrid,
Thought gets dry in the brain.

There is that woman again:
"Strawberries! fourpence a pottle!"
Thought gets dry in the brain;
Ink gets dry in the bottle.

"Strawberries! fourpence a pottle!"
Oh for the green of a lane!—
Ink gets dry in the bottle;
"Buzz" goes a fly in the pane!

Oh for the green of a lane,
Where one might lie and be lazy!
"Buzz" goes a fly in the pane;
Bluebottles drive me crazy!

Where one might lie and be lazy,
Careless of Town and all in it!—
Bluebottles drive me crazy:
I shall go mad in a minute!

Careless of Town and all in it,
With some one to soothe and to still you,
I shall go mad in a minute,
Bluebottle, then I shall kill you!

With some one to soothe and to still you,
As only one's feminine kin do,—
Bluebottle, then I shall kill you:
There now! I've broken the window!

As only one's feminine kin do,—
Some muslin-clad Mabel or May!—
There now! I've broken the window!
Bluebottle's off and away!

Some muslin-clad Mabel or May,
To dash one with *eau de Cologne;*—
Bluebottle's off and away,
And why should I stay here alone?

To dash one with *eau de Cologne,*
All over one's eminent forehead;
And why should I stay here alone?
Toiling in Town now is "horrid."

Austin Dobson.

WHEN I SAW YOU LAST, ROSE

WHEN I saw you last, Rose,
You were only so high;—
How fast the time goes!

Like a bud ere it blows,
You just peeped at the sky,
When I saw you last, Rose!

Now your petals unclose,
Now your May-time is nigh;—
How fast the time goes!

And a life—how it grows!
You were scarcely so shy,
When I saw you last, Rose!

In your bosom it shows
There's a guest on the sly;
How fast the time goes!

Is it Cupid? Who knows!
Yet you used not to sigh,
When I saw you last, Rose;—
How fast the time goes!

Austin Dobson.

TO "LYDIA LANGUISH"

"Il me faut des emotions."—BLANCHE AMORY

YOU ask me, Lydia, "whether I,
If you refuse my suit, shall die,"
(Now pray don't let this hurt you!)
Although the time be out of joint,
I should not think a bodkin's point
The sole resource of virtue;
Nor shall I, though your mood endure,
Attempt a final Water-cure
Except against my wishes;
For I respectfully decline
To dignify the Serpentine,
And make *hors-d'œuvres* for fishes;
But if you ask me whether I
Composedly can go,
Without a look, without a sigh,
Why, then I answer—No.

"You are assured," you sadly say
(If in this most considerate way
To treat my suit your will is),
That I shall "quickly find as fair
Some new Neæra's tangled hair—
Some easier Amaryllis."
I cannot promise to be cold
If smiles are kind as yours of old
On lips of later beauties;
Nor can I, if I would, forget

The homage that is Nature's debt,
While man has social duties;
But if you ask shall I prefer
To you I honour so,
A somewhat visionary Her,
I answer truly—No.

You fear, you frankly add, "to find
In me too late the altered mind
That altering Time estranges."
To this I make response that we
(As physiologists agree)
Must have septennial changes;
This is a thing beyond control,
And it were best upon the whole
To try and find out whether
We could not, by some means, arrange
This not-to-be-avoided change
So as to change together:
But, had you asked me to allow
That you could ever grow
Less amiable than you are now,—
Emphatically—No.

But—to be serious—if you care
To know how I shall really bear
This much-discussed rejection,
I answer you. As feeling men
Behave, in best romances, when
You outrage their affection;—
With that gesticulatory woe,

By which, as melodramas show,
Despair is indicated;
Enforced by all the liquid grief
Which hugest pocket-handkerchief
Has ever simulated;
And when, arrived so far, you say
In tragic accents "Go,"
Then, Lydia, then . . . I still shall stay,
And firmly answer—No.

Austin Dobson.

THE OLD SEDAN CHAIR

IT stands in the stable-yard, under the eaves,
Propped up by a broom-stick and covered with leaves:
It once was the pride of the gay and the fair,
But now 'tis a ruin,—that old Sedan chair!

It is battered and tattered,—it little avails
That once it was lacquered, and glistened with nails;
For its leather is cracked into lozenge and square,
Like a canvas by Wilkie,—that old Sedan chair!

See,—here came the bearing-straps; here were the holes
For the poles of the bearers—when once there were poles;
It was cushioned with silk, it was wadded with hair,
As the birds have discovered,—that old Sedan chair!

"Where's Troy?" says the poet! Look,—under the seat,
Is a nest with four eggs,—'tis the favored retreat
Of the Muscovy hen, who has hatched, I dare swear,
Quite an army of chicks in that old Sedan chair!

And yet—can't you fancy a face in the frame
Of the window,—some high-headed damsel or dame,
Be-patched and be-powdered, just set by the stair,
While they raise up the lid of that old Sedan chair?

Can't you fancy Sir Plume, as beside her he stands,
With his ruffles a-droop on his delicate hands,
With his cinnamon coat, with his laced solitaire,
As he lifts her out light from that old Sedan chair?

Then it swings away slowly. Ah, many a league
It has trotted 'twixt sturdy-legged Terence and Teague;

Stout fellows!—but prone, on a question of fare,
To brandish the poles of that old Sedan chair!

It has waited by portals where Garrick has played;
It has waited by Heidegger's "Grand Masquerade";
For my Lady Codille, for my Lady Bellair,
It has waited—and waited, that old Sedan chair!

Oh, the scandals it knows! Oh, the tales it could tell
Of Drum and Ridotto, of Rake and of Belle,—
Of Cock-fight and Levee, and (scarcely more rare!)
Of Fête-days at Tyburn, that old Sedan chair!

"Heu! *quantum mutata*," I say as I go.
It deserves better fate than a stable-yard, though!
We must furbish it up, and dispatch it—"With care,"—
To a Fine-Art Museum—that old Sedan chair!

Austin Dobson.

"LE ROMAN DE LA ROSE"

POOR Rose! I lift you from the street,—
Far better I should own you
Than you should lie for random feet
Where careless hands have thrown you.

Poor pinky petals, crushed and torn!
Did heartless Mayfair use you,
Then cast you forth to lie forlorn,
For chariot-wheels to bruise you?

I saw you last in Edith's hair,
Rose, you would scarce discover
That I she passed upon the stair
Was Edith's favoured lover.

A month—"a little month"—ago—
O theme for moral writer!—
'Twixt you and me, my Rose, you know,
She might have been politer;

But let that pass. She gave you then—
Behind the oleander—
To one, perhaps, of all the men—
Who best could understand her,—

Cyril, that, duly flattered, took,
As only Cyril's able,
With just the same Arcadian look
He used, last night, for Mabel;

Then, having waltzed till every star
Had paled away in morning,

Lit up his cynical cigar,
And tossed you downward, scorning.

Kismet, my Rose! Revenge is sweet,—
She made my heart strings quiver;
And yet—You sha'n't lie in the street;
I'll drop you in the river.

Austin Dobson.

NINETY-NINE IN THE SHADE

O FOR a lodge in a garden of cucumbers!
O for an iceberg or two at control!
O for a vale which at mid-day the dew cumbers!
O for a pleasure-trip up to the pole!

O for a little one-story thermometer,
With nothing but zeroes all ranged in a row!
O for a big double-barreled hygrometer,
To measure this moisture that rolls from my brow!

O that this cold world were twenty times colder!
(That's irony red-hot, it seemeth to me);
O for a turn of its dreaded cold shoulder!
O what a comfort an ague would be!

O for a grotto frost-lined and rill-riven,
Scooped in the rock under cataract vast!
O for a winter of discontent even!
O for wet blankets judiciously cast!

O for a soda-fount spouting up boldly
From every hot lamp-post against the hot sky!
O for proud maiden to look on me coldly,
Freezing my soul with a glance of her eye!

Then O for a draught from a cup of cold pizen,
And O for a resting-place in the cold grave!
With a bath in the Styx where the thick shadow lies on
And deepens the chill of its dark-running wave.

Rossiter Johnson.

BRIGHTON PIER

WHICH is the merriest place to love,
Whether it be for a day or year;
Where can we slip, like a cast-off glove,
The care that hovers our world above?
Come and be taught upon Brighton Pier!

Wandering waves on the shingle dash,
The sky's too blue for a thoughtless tear;
Danger is nothing but pessimist trash,
And the morning's made for a healthy splash:
Come for a header from Brighton Pier!

Filled with life, see the children race,
Motherly hearts they quake with fear,
Meeting the breezes face to face!
Whether we're steady or "go the pace,"
Let us be young upon Brighton Pier!

Here she comes with her love-lit eyes,
Hearts will throb when a darling's near;
Would it be well to avoid her—wise?
Every fool in the wide world tries,
But love must win upon Brighton Pier!

Lazily lost in a dream we sit—
Maidens' eyes are a waveless mere—
There's many a vow when seagulls flit,
And many a sigh when lamps are lit,
And many a kiss upon Brighton Pier.

Dear old friends of the days long fled,

Why did you vanish and leave me here?
Girls are marrying, boys are wed,
Youth is living, but I seem dead,
Kicking my heels upon Brighton Pier!

Clement Scott.

A CONTRADICTION

"Varium et mutabile semper Fœmina!"—VIRGIL

THEY say she's like an April day,
All sun and shower, grave and gay,
Just half in love, and half in play,
Like other misses.
Go to! They tell a pack of lies;
For I have heard her heart-drawn sighs,
And I have seen her inmost eyes,
And felt her kisses!

They think her laugh is over-bold,
And hint her smiles are bought for gold;
Dull heretics have thought her cold,
As is the fashion.
Ah me! when we together stole
Across the weald to leafy Knole,
'Twas there she showed to me her soul
And all her passion!

They vow her life is tossed about
From ball to picnic, play to rout;
A careless butterfly, no doubt,
That scandal crushes.
What could we answer, if 'twere said
That Time and Fate two lovers led
To lily-streams at Maidenhead,
Among the rushes?

Her reputation shivered most

Last night at supper, when our host
Made her of careless lips the toast
And reigning goddess.
But I, who know my love, dare say
She thought of home, and tried to pray
Before her handmaid slipped away
Her satin bodice.

Your silly worldings all forget
Her depth of hidden life, and bet
They've never met her equal yet
In fact or fiction.
But I, who love in secret, sit
Unweaving webs that Fate has knit
To bind me to so exquisite
A contradiction.

Clement Scott.

RONDEL

KISS me, sweetheart; the Spring is here
And Love is Lord of you and me.
The blue-bells beckon each passing bee;
The wild wood laughs to the flowered year:
There is no bird in brake or brere,
But to his little mate sings he,
"Kiss me, sweetheart; the Spring is here,
And Love is Lord of you and me!"

The blue sky laughs out sweet and clear,
The missel-thrush upon the tree
Pipes for sheer gladness loud and free;
And I go singing to my dear,
"Kiss me, sweetheart; the Spring is here,
And Love is Lord of you and me."

John Payne.

WHITE, PILLARED NECK

I

WHITE, pillared neck; a brow to make men quake;
A woman's perfect form;
Like some cool marble, should that wake,
Breathe, and be warm.

II

A shape, a mind, a heart
Of womanhood the whole;
Her breath, her smile, her touch, her art,
All—save her soul.

Richard Watson Gilder.

JANET

I

I REMEMBER
That November
When the new November child
On this old world woke and smiled.

II

Here's a woman,
Sweet and human,
And they call her Janet, now,—
I can't make it out, I vow

III

It only seems
One night of dreams;
Years they say; how *do* they plan it?
What's become of Little Janet?

IV

Never mind;
She's good; she's kind;
Age can never bend or win her;
There's a heart of youth within her.

Richard Watson Gilder.

FOR A FAN

EACH of us answers to a call;

Master or mistress have we all.

I belong to lovely Anne;

Dost thou wish *thou* wert a fan?

Thus to be treasured, thus to be prest,

Pleasuring thus, and thus caressed?

Richard Watson Gilder.

BALLADE OF SUMMER

WHEN strawberry pottles are common and cheap,
Ere elms be black, or limes be sere,
When midnight dances are murdering sleep,
Then comes in the sweet o' the year
And far from Fleet Street, far from here,
The Summer is Queen in the length of the land,
And moonlit nights they are soft and clear,
When fans for a penny are sold in the Strand!

When clamour that doves in the lindens keep
Mingles with musical plash of the weir,
Where drowned green tresses of crowsfeet creep,
Then comes in the sweet o' the year!
And better a crust and a beaker of beer,
With rose hung hedges on either hand,
Than a palace in town and a prince's cheer,
When fans for a penny are sold in the Strand!

When big trout late in the twilight leap,
When cuckoo clamoureth far and near,
When glittering scythes in the hayfield reap,
Then comes in the sweet o' the year!
And it's oh to sail, with the wind to steer,
While kine knee-deep in the water stand,
On a highland loch, on a Lowland mere,
When fans for a penny are sold in the Strand!

ENVOY

Friend, with the fops while we dawdle here,

Then comes in the sweet o' the year!
And the summer runs out, like grains of sand,
When fans for a penny are sold in the Strand!

Andrew Lang.

COLINETTE

FRANCE your country, as we know;
Room enough for guessing yet,
What lips now or long ago,
Kissed and named you—Colinette.
In what fields from sea to sea,
By what stream your home was set,
Loire or Seine was glad of thee,
Marne or Rhone, O Colinette?

Did you stand with "maidens ten,
Fairer maids were never seen,"
When the young king and his men
Passed among the orchards green?
Nay, old ballads have a note
Mournful we would fain forget;
No such sad old air should float
Round your young brows, Colinette.

Say, did Ronsard sing to you.
Shepherdess to lull his pain,
When the court went wandering through
Rose pleasances of Touraine?
Ronsard and his famous Rose
Long are dust the breezes fret;
You, within the garden close,
You are blooming, Colinette.

Have I seen you proud and gay,
With a patched and perfumed beau,
Dancing through the summer day,

Misty summer of Watteau?
Nay, so sweet a maid as you
Never walked a minuet
With the splendid courtly crew;
Nay, forgive me, Colinette.

Not from Greuze's canvases
Do you cast a glance, a smile;
You are not as one of these,
Yours is beauty without guile.
Round your maiden brows and hair
Maidenhood and Childhood met,
Crown and kiss you, sweet and fair,
New art's blossom, Colinette.

Andrew Lang.

BALLADE OF DEAD LADIES
(After Villon)

NAY, tell me now in what strange air
The Roman Flora dwells to-day;
Where Archippiada hides, and where
Beautiful Thais has passed away?
Whence answers Echo, afield, astray,
By mere or stream,—around, below?
Lovelier she than a woman of clay;
Nay, but where is the last year's snow?

Where is wise Héloise, that care
Brought on Abeilard, and dismay?
All for her love he found a snare,
A maimed poor monk in orders grey;
And where's the Queen who willed to slay
Buridan, that in a sack must go
Afloat down Seine,—a perilous way—
Nay, but where is the last year's snow?

Where's that White Queen, a lily rare,
With her sweet song, the Siren's lay?
Where's Bertha Broad-foot, Beatrice fair?
Alys and Ermengarde, where are they?
Good Joan, whom English did betray
In Rouen town, and burned her? No,
Maiden and Queen, no man may say;
Nay, but where is the last year's snow?

ENVOY

Prince, all this week thou need'st not pray,

Nor yet this year the thing to know.
One burden answers, ever and aye,
"Nay, but where is the last year's snow?"
Andrew Lang.

IL BACIO

KISS! Hollyhock in Love's luxuriant close!
Brisk music played on pearly little keys;
In tempo with the witching melodies
Love in the ardent heart repeating goes.

Sonorous, graceful Kiss, hail! Kiss divine!
Unequalled boon, unutterable bliss!
Man, bent o'er thine enthralling chalice, Kiss,
Grows drunken with a rapture only thine!

Thou comfortest as music does, and wine,
And grief dies smothered in thy purple fold.
Let one greater than I, Kiss, and more bold,
Rear thee a classic, monumental line.

Humble Parisian bard, this infantile
Bouquet of rhymes I tender half in fear. . . .
Be gracious, and in guerdon, on the dear
Red lips of One I know, a light and smile!

Paul Verlaine.

SUR L'HERBE

"THE abbé rambles."—"You, marquis,
Have put your wig on all awry."—
"This wine of Cypress kindles me
Less, my Camargo, than your eye!"

"My passion"—"Do, mi, sol, la, si."—
"Abbé, your villainy lies bare."—
"Mesdames, I climb up yonder tree
And fetch a star down, I declare."

"Let each kiss his own lady, then
The others."—"Would that I were, too,
A lap-dog!"—"Softly, gentlemen!"—
"Do, mi."—"The moon!—Hey, how d'ye do?"

Paul Verlaine.

THE ROMANCE OF A GLOVE

HERE on my desk it lies,
Here as the daylight dies,
One small glove just her size—
Six and a quarter;
Pearly gray, a colour neat,
Deux boutons all complete,
Faint scented, soft and sweet;
Could glove be smarter?

Can I the day forget,
Years ago, when the pet
Gave it me?—where we met
Still I remember;
Then 'twas the summer time;
Now as I write this rhyme
Children love pantomime—
'Tis December.

Fancy my boyish bliss
Then when she gave me this,
And how the frequent kiss
Crumpled its fingers;
Then she was fair and kind,
Now, when I've changed my mind,
Still some scent undefined
On the glove lingers.

Though she's a matron sage,
Yet I have kept the gage;
While, as I pen this page,

Still comes a goddess,
Her eldest daughter, fair,
With the same eyes and hair;
Happy the arm I swear,
That clasps her bodice.

Heaven grant her fate be bright,
And her step ever light
As it will be to-night,
First in the dances.
Why did her mother prove
False when I dared to love?
Zounds! I shall burn the glove!
This my romance is.

H. Savile Clarke.

IF

OH, if the world were mine, Love,
I'd give the world for thee!
Alas! there is no sign, Love,
Of that contingency.

Were I a king—which isn't
To be considered now,—
A diadem had glistened
Upon thy lovely brow.

Had fame with laurels crowned me,—
She hasn't up to date,—
Nor time nor change had found me
To love and thee ingrate.

If death threw down his gage, Love,
Though Life is dear to me,
I'd die, e'en of old age, Love,
To win a smile from thee.

But being poor we part, Dear,
And love, sweet love, must die,—
Thou wilt not break thy heart, Dear;
No more, I think, shall I.

James Jeffrey Roche.

DON'T

YOUR eyes were made for laughter,
Sorrow befits them not;
Would you be blithe hereafter,
Avoid the lover's lot.

The rose and lily blended
Possess your cheeks so fair;
Care never was intended
To leave his furrows there.

Your heart was not created
To fret itself away,
Being unduly mated
To common human clay.

But hearts were made for loving,—
Confound philosophy!
Forget what I've been proving,
Sweet Phyllis, and love me.

James Jeffrey Roche.

ON REREADING TÉLÉMAQUE

"Calypso could not console herself"

I PLACE thee back upon the shelf,
O Fénelon, how scant thy knowledge,
Who seemed as Solomon himself
To me, a callow youth at college!

No need to say thou wert a priest;
No need to own that I am human;
Mine this advantage is—at least
I've learned the alphabet of Woman.

And yet but half the truth is told:
I do thee wrong, sagacious Mentor,—
Calypso could not be consoled
Until another man was sent her!

James Jeffrey Roche.

VALENTINE

GREAT Antony, I drink to thee,
The Roman lover bold,
Who knew the worth of love and earth
And gave the dross for gold.

Rich Antony, I envy thee,
Who hadst a world to stake,
And, win or lose, didst bravely choose
To risk it for Her sake.

Poor Antony, I pity thee,
So small a world was thine,
I'd scorn to lay the prize to-day
Before my Valentine!

James Jeffrey Roche.

BIFTEK AUX CHAMPIGNONS

MIMI, do you remember—
Don't get behind your fan—
That morning in September
On the cliffs of Grand Manan,
Where to the shock of Fundy
The topmost harebells sway
(*Campanula rotundi—
folia: cf.* Gray)?

On the pastures high and level,
That overlook the sea,
Where I wondered what the devil
Those little things could be
That Mimi stooped to gather,
As she strolled across the down,
And held her dress skirt rather—
Oh, now, you needn't frown.

For you know the dew was heavy,
And your boots, I know, were thin;
So a little extra brevi-
ty in skirts was sure, no sin.
Besides, who minds a cousin?
First, second, even third,—
I've kissed 'em by the dozen,
And they never once demurred.

"If one's allowed to ask it,"
Quoth I, "*Ma belle cousine*,
What have you in your basket?"

Those baskets white and green
The brave Passamaquoddies
Weave out of scented grass,
And sell to tourist bodies
Who through Mt. Desert pass.

You answered, slightly frowning,
"Put down your stupid book—
That everlasting Browning!—
And come and help me look,
Mushroom you spik him English,
I call him *champignon:*
I'll teach you to distinguish
The right kind from the wrong."

There was no fog on Fundy
That blue September day;
The west wind, for that one day,
Had swept it all away.
The lighthouse glasses twinkled,
The white gulls screamed and flew,
The merry sheep-bells tinkled,
The merry breezes blew.

The bayberry aromatic,
The papery immortelles
(That give our grandma's attic
That sentimental smell,
Tied up in little brush-brooms)
Were sweet as new-mown hay,
While we went hunting mushrooms

That blue September day.

Henry Augustin Beers.

AN EXPLANATION

HER lips were so near
That what—else could I do?
You'll be angry, I fear,
But her lips were so near—
Well, I can't make it clear,
Or explain it to you,
But—her lips were so near
That—what else could I do?

Walter Learned.

MARJORIE'S KISSES

MARJORIE laughs and climbs on my knee,
And I kiss her and she kisses me,
I kiss her, but I don't much care,
Because, although she is charming and fair,
Marjorie's only three.

But there will come a time, I ween,
When, if I tell her of this little scene,
She will smile and prettily blush, and then
I shall long in vain to kiss her again,
When Marjorie's seventeen.

Walter Learned.

MISS NANCY'S GOWN

IN days when George the Third was King
And ruled the Old Dominion,
And Law and Fashion owned the sway
Of Parliament's opinion,
A good ship brought across the sea
A treasure fair and fine,—
Miss Nancy's gown from London Town,
The latest Court design!

The plaited waist from neck to belt
Scarce measured half a span;
The sleeves, balloon-like, at the top
Could hold her feather fan;
The narrow skirt with bias gore
Revealed an ankle neat,
Whene'er she put her dainty foot
From carriage step to street!

By skilful hands this wondrous gown
Of costliest stuff was made,
Cocoons of France on Antwerp looms
Wrought to embossed brocade,
Where roses red and violets
In blooming beauty grew,
As if young May were there alway,
And June and April too!

And from this bower of delight
Miss Nancy reigned a Queen,
Nor one disloyal heart rebelled

In all her wild demesne:
The noble House of Burgesses
Forgot its fierce debate
O'er rights of Crown, when Nancy's gown
Appeared in Halls of State!

Through jocund reel, or measured tread
Of stately minuet,
Like fairy vision shone the bloom
Of rose and violet,
As, hand in hand with Washington,
The hero of the day,
The smiling face and nymph-like grace
Of Nancy led the way!

A century, since that gay time
The merry dance was trod,
Has passed, and Nancy long has slept
Beneath the churchyard sod;
Yet on the brocade velvet gown
The rose and violet
Are blooming bright as on the night
She danced the minuet!

Zitella Cocke.

"LE DERNIER JOUR D'UN CONDAMNÉ"

OLD coat, for some three or four seasons
We've been jolly comrades, but now
We part, old companion, forever;
To fate, and the fashion, I bow.
You'd look well enough at a dinner,
I'd wear you with pride at a ball;
But I'm dressing to-night for a wedding—
My own—and you'd not do at all.

You've too many wine-stains about you,
You're scented too much with cigars,
When the gaslight shines full on your collar
It glitters with myriad stars,
That wouldn't look well at my wedding;
They'd seem inappropriate there—
Nell doesn't use diamond powder.
She tells me it ruins the hair.

You've been out on Cozzen's piazza
Too late, when the evenings were damp,
When the moon-beams were silvering Cro'nest,
And the lights were all out in the camp.
You've rested on highly-oiled stairways
Too often, when sweet eyes were bright.
And somebody's ball dress—not Nellie's—
Flowed 'round you in rivers of white.

There's a reprobate looseness about you;
Should I wear you to-night, I believe,
As I come with my bride from the altar,

You'd laugh in your wicked old sleeve,
When you felt there the tremulous pressure
Of her hand, in its delicate glove,
That is telling me shyly, but proudly,
Her trust is as deep as her love.

So, go to your grave in the wardrobe,
And furnish a feast for the moth,
Nell's glove shall betray its sweet secrets
To younger, more innocent cloth.
'Tis time to put on your successor—
It's made in a fashion that's new;
Old coat, I'm afraid it will never
Sit as easily on me as you.

George A. Baker.

MY WOOING

ONE evening, many months ago,
We two conversed together;
It must have been in June or so,
For sultry was the weather.
The waving branches made the ground
With lights and shadows quiver;
We sat upon a grassy mound
That overhung a river.

We thought, as you've perhaps inferred,
Our destinies of linking:
But neither of us spoke a word,
For each of us was thinking.
Her ma had lands at Skibbereen,
Her pa estates in Devon;
And she was barely seventeen,
And I was thirty-seven.

We gathered blossoms from the bank,
And in the water flung them:
We watched them as they rose and sank
With flakes of foam among them.
As towards the falls in mimic face
They sailed—these heads of clover—
We watched them quicken in their pace,
We watched them tumble over.

We watched them; and our calm repose
Seemed calmer for their troubles;
We watched them as they sank and rose

And battled with the bubbles.
We noticed then a little bird,
Down at the margin, drinking:
But neither of us spoke a word,
For each of us was thinking.

At length I thought I fairly might
Declare my passion frantic:
(The scenery, I'm sure, was quite
Sufficiently romantic.)
I'd heard a proverb short and quaint
My memory—though shady—
Informed me it began with "faint,"
And finished up with "lady."

I summoned then the pluck to speak:
(I felt I'd have to, one day,
I only saw her once a week,
And this was only Monday.)
I called her angel, duck, and dove,
I said I loved her dearly,
My words—the whisperings of Love—
Were eloquent, or nearly.

I told her that my heart was true,
And constant as the river:
I said, "I'll love you as I do,
'For ever and for ever!'
Oh! let me hear that voice divine—"
I stopped a bit and listened;
I murmured then, "Be mine, be mine,"

She said, "I won't!"—and isn't.

Edwin Hamilton.

WINTRY PARIS

OH, the dingy winter days!
Oh, the woven blues and greys!
Oh, the drizzles and the puddles and the freezing!
Nippy Paris to New York
Is a sinker to a cork
Superstition and tradition all her pleasing.

Oh, the glacial Gallic gloom
In a candle-darkened room
Sends the spirit of a Gothamite to zero
When I found the fire dead
And sped shuddering to bed.
How I longed to dream of burning Rome and Nero!

Don't believe them when they say
The Parisians all are gay;
Not a capital where gaiety so rare is.
Why, I positively think
My Manhattan blues are pink
When contrasted with the blues I had in Paris.

Anonymous.

THE ROSE

MY Lilla gave me yestermorn
A rose, methinks in Eden born,
And as she gave it, little elf!
She blush'd like any rose herself.
Then said I, full of tenderness,
"Since this sweet rose I owe to you,
Dear girl, why may I not possess
The lovelier Rose that gave it too?"

Anonymous.

INDECISION

DO I love her?
Dimpling red lips at me pouting,
Dimpling shoulders at me flouting;
No, I don't!

Do I love her?
'Prisoned in those crystal eyes
Purity forever lies;
Yes, I do!

Do I love her?
Little, wild and wilful fiction,
Teasing, torturing contradiction;
No, I don't!

Do I love her?
With kind acts and sweet words she
Aids and comforts poverty;
Yes, I do!

Do I love her?
Quick she puts her cuirass on,
Stabs with laughter, stings with scorn;
No, I don't!

Do I love her?
No! Then to my arms she flies,
Filling me with glad surprise;
Ah, yes I do!

Anonymous.

LOGIC

I. HER RESPECTABLE PAPA'S

"MY Dear, be sensible. Upon my word,
This—for a woman even—is absurd.
His income's not a hundred pounds, I know.
He's not worth loving."—"But I love him so."

II. HER MOTHER'S

"You silly child, he is well made and tall;
But looks are far from being all in all.
His social standing's low, his family's low,
He's not worth loving."—"And I love him so."

III. HER ETERNAL FRIEND'S

"Is that he picking up the fallen fan?
My Dear! he's such an awkward, ugly man!
You must be certain, pet, to answer 'No.'
He's not worth loving."—"And I love him so."

IV. HER BROTHER'S

"By Jove, were I a girl—thro' horrid hap—
I wouldn't have a milk-and-water chap.
The man has not a single spark of 'go,'
He's not worth loving."—"Yet, I love him so."

V. HER OWN

"And were he everything to which I've listened;
Though he were ugly, awkward (and he isn't)—
Poor, low-born, and destitute of 'go,'

He is worth loving, for I love him so!"

Punch.

CONVERSATIONAL

"HOW'S your father?" came the whisper,
Bashful Ned the silence breaking;
"Oh, he's nicely," Annie murmured,
Smilingly the question taking.

Conversation flagged a moment,
Hopeless Ned essayed another:
"Annie, I—I," then a coughing,
And the question, "How's your mother?"

"Mother? Oh, she's doing finely!"
Fleeting fast was all forbearance,
When in low, despairing accents,
Came the climax, "How's your parents?"

Anonymous.

IF YOU WANT A KISS, WHY, TAKE IT

THERE'S a jolly Saxon proverb
That is pretty much like this—
That a man is half in heaven
If he has a woman's kiss.
There is danger in delaying,
For the sweetness may forsake it;
So I tell you, bashful lover,
If you want a kiss, why, take it.

Never let another fellow
Steal a march on you in this;
Never let a laughing maiden
See you spoiling for a kiss.
There's a royal way to kissing,
And the jolly ones who make it
Have a motto that is winning,—
If you want a kiss, why, take it.

Any fool may face a cannon,
Anybody wear a crown,
But a man must win a woman
If he'd have her for his own.
Would you have the golden apple,
You must find the tree and shake it;
If the thing is worth the having,
And you want a kiss, why take it.

Who would burn upon a desert
With a forest smiling by?
Who would change his sunny summer

For a bleak and wintry sky?
Oh, I tell you there is magic,
And you cannot, cannot break it;
For the sweetest part of loving
Is to want a kiss, and take it.

Anonymous.

EDUCATIONAL COURTSHIP

SHE was a Boston maiden, and she'd scarcely passed eighteen,
And as lovely as an houri, but of grave and sober mien,
A sweet encyclopædia of every kind of lore,
Though love looked coyly from behind the glasses that she wore.

She sat beside her lover, with her elbow on his knee,
And dreamily she gazed upon the slumbering summer sea,
Until he broke the silence, saying, "Pray, Minerva, dear,
Inform me of the meaning of the Thingness of the Here?

"I know you're just from Concord, where the lights of wisdom be,
Your head crammed full to bursting with their philosophy,—
Those hairy-headed sages and maids of hosiery blue;
Then solve me the conundrum, love, that I have put to you."

She smiled a dreamy smile, and said, "The Thingness of the Here
Is that which is not passed and hasn't yet arrived, my dear.
Indeed," the maid continued, with a calm, unruffled brow,
"The Thingness of the Here is just the Thingness of the Now."

A smile illumed the lover's face; then, without undue haste,
He slid a manly arm around the maiden's slender waist,
And on her cherry lips impressed a warm and loving kiss,
And said, "Love, this is what I call the Nowness of the This."

Anonymous.

KISSING'S NO SIN

SOME say that kissing's a sin;
But I think it's nane ava,
For kissing has wonn'd in this warld
Since ever there was twa.

O, if it wasna lawfu'
Lawyers wadna allow it;
If it wasna holy,
Ministers wadna do it.

If it wasna modest,
Maidens wadna tak' it;
If it wasna plenty,
Puir folks wadna get it.

Anonymous.

THE BEST THING IN THE WORLD

WHAT'S the best thing in the world?
June-rose, by May-dew impearled;
Sweet south-wind, that means no rain;
Truth, not cruel to a friend;
Pleasure, not in haste to end;
Beauty, not self-decked and curled
Till its pride is over-plain;
Light, that never makes you wink;
Memory, that gives no pain;
Love, when, *so*, you're loved again.
What's the best thing in the world?—
Something out of it, I think.

Anonymous.

HER NEIGHBOURS

THEY lingered at her father's door,
The moon was shining bright,
And to the maiden o'er and o'er
The youth had said, "Good night."

But still reluctant to depart,
Her tiny hand he pressed,
While all the love that filled his heart
His ardent looks confessed.

At length she closer to him crept,
Her eyes upon him bent,
And softly asked, "How have you kept,
Thus far, the fast of Lent?"

He smiled, and, as a manly arm
Around her waist he threw,
He said, "I've done no neighbour harm—
Pray, tell me, how have you?"

"Oh! better far, I'm sure," she said,
The charming little elf.
"I've loved (she blushed and bent her head)
My neighbour as myself."

"Who is your neighbour?" questioned he,
As to his breast he drew
The gentle maid, and blushing, she
With one word answered—"You."

Anonymous.

TO CELIA

(Who refuses to be drawn into an argument)

DEAR, if you carelessly agree,
With that so irritating air,
To every word that falls from me—
Dear, if you care

To drive a lover to despair
With bland "Oh, yes," and "Ah, I see,"—
Why, do it, if you like—so there!

It vindicates my theory
No woman's wise as well as fair;
And yet . . . how clever you can be,
Dear, if you care!

E. H. Lacon Watson.

IN FOR IT

I ROSE betimes, and donned a suit
Of clothes, whose fit immaculate
Was not a question for dispute,
Whose cut was far above debate.
I breakfasted, or rather tried,
But strange my appetite behaving,
A., B. and S. alone supplied
My feeble craving.

I fidgeted about the place,
I smoothed my hat some twenty times,
I almost cursed the clock's slow pace
And listened for the neighb'ring chimes—
I stretched my gloves—they were a pair
Of lemon kids, extremely "fetching";
And so I used peculiar care
About the stretching.

'Twas past eleven when my friend
Arrived, and took me 'neath his wing,
For he had promised to attend
Upon me kindly, and "to bring
Me smiling to the scratch," as he
Was pleased to term it, being merry,
'Twas quite another thing with me;
'Twas diff'rent, very.

We drove to Church, and there I found
Myself the object of each gaze;
I hardly dared to look around,

I felt completely in a maze—
We had to wait, I dropped my hat,
Then split a glove in very flurry,
Grew hot, and wished devoutly that
The rest would hurry.

When all was o'er, we had to face
A grinning crowd's rude gaping stare,
I strove to don unconscious grace,
And look as if I didn't care—
We braved it out, got home, and then
There came a plethora of kissin':
Of course I took good care the men
Did not join this in.

We next were victims of a meal,
A melancholy sad pretence,
And I thereat was made to feel
How hard it is to utter sense:
The carriage came at last, and we
For not a single moment tarried,
And driving off, it dawned on me
That I was married.

Somerville Gibney.

KIRTLE RED

A DAMSEL fair, on a summer's day—
—Sing heigh, sing ho, for the summer!
Sat under a tree in a kirtle gray,
Singing, "Somebody's late at tryst to-day;
Gather ye rosebuds while ye may,
Or the leaves may fall in summer!"

Answered a little bird overhead—
As birds will do in summer;
"Some body *has* kept tryst," it said,
"With somebody else in a kirtle red,
And they are going to be marrièd."
Sing heigh, sing ho, for the summer!

"With all my heart, little bird," said she;
Sing heigh, sing ho, for the summer!
"He's welcome to kirtle red for me;
Somebody's fast, while somebody's free!
There's nothing, no, nothing, like libertie!"
—Sing heigh, sing ho, for the summer!

W. H. Bellamy.

A BAGATELLE

A BAGATELLE! Ah, Mistress Prue,
So gaily laughing all life through,
You call it that, the flower you fling
Lightly aside, the song you sing,
The fan, the glove no longer new.

But to your careless eyes of blue
A bow, a heart that's fond and true,
Is, like your glove, that worthless thing—
A bagatelle.

While I who prize your glove, your shoe,
The rose that o'er your lips you drew,
Hold worthless spring's fresh blossoming,
Hold worthless life's whole offering,
Because my love is but to you
A bagatelle.

James G. Burnett.

A LOVE TEST

SWEET, do you ask me if you love or no?
Soon will your answers to my questions show:
If in your cheeks hot blushes come and go,
Like rose-leaves shaken on new-fallen snow;
If tender sorrows in your heart arise,
And sudden teardrops tremble in your eyes;
If from my presence you would sigh to part,
Believe me, darling, I have touched your heart.

If when I speak your blue-veined eyelids sink,
And veil the thoughts you scarcely dare to think:
If when I greet you, hardly you reply,
And when we part, but breathe a faint "Good-bye!"
If your sweet face to mine you cannot raise,
Yet fear not so to meet another's gaze;
If all these things to make you glad combine,
Believe me, darling, that your heart is mine.

Carl Herlozssohn.

THE MISTAKEN MOTH

'MID the summer flush of roses
Red and white,
Sat a damsel fair, a very
Pretty sight;
Till a butterfly, so smart,
With a flutter and a dart,
Kissed her mouth and made her start
In a fright.

"Ah, forgive me!" begged the insect,
"If you please;
I assure you that I didn't
Mean to tease.
I but took your rosebud lip
For the rose wherein I dip,
All its honey sweet to sip
At mine ease."

Said the beauty, to the moth,
"You may try
To excuse your forward conduct,
Sir, but I
Wish it clearly understood
That such roses are too good
To be kissed by every rude
Butterfly!"

Translated from Wegener.

MY PRETTY NEIGHBOR

IF you've nothing, dear, to tell me,
Why, each morning passing by,
With your sudden smiles compel me,
To adore you, then repel me,
Pretty little neighbor, why?
Why if you have naught to tell me,
Do you so my patience try?

If you've nothing sweet to teach me,
Tell me why you press my hand?
I'll attend if you'll impeach me
Of my sins, or even preach me
Sermons hard to understand;
But if you have naught to teach me,
Dear, your meaning I demand!

If you wish me, love, to leave you,
Why forever walk my way?
Then, when gladly I receive you,
Wherefore do I seem to grieve you?
Must I then, in truth, believe you
Wish me, darling, far away?
Do you wish me, love, to leave you?
Pretty little neighbor, say!

Translated from Wegener.

IF

IF a man could live a thousand years,
When half his life had passed,
He might, by strict economy,
A fortune have amassed.

Then having gained some common-sense,
And knowledge, too, of life,
He could select the woman who
Would make him a true wife.

But as it is, man hasn't time
To even pay his debts,
And weds to be acquainted with
The woman whom he gets.

H. C. Dodge.

TO MISTRESS PYRRHA

WHAT perfumed, posie-dizened sirrah,
With smiles for diet,
Clasps you, O fair but faithless Pyrrha,
On the quiet?
For whom do you bind up your tresses,
As spun-gold yellow,—
Meshes that go with your caresses,
To snare a fellow?

How will he rail at fate capricious,
And curse you duly,
Yet now he deems your wiles delicious,—
You perfect, truly!
Pyrrha, your love's a treacherous ocean;
He'll soon fall in there!
Then shall I gloat on his commotion,
For I have been there!

Eugene Field.

THE TEA-GOWN

MY lady has a tea-gown
That is wondrous fair to see,—
It is flounced and ruffed and plaited and puffed,
As a tea-gown ought to be;
And I thought she must be jesting
Last night at supper when
She remarked by chance, that it came from France,
And had cost but two pounds ten.

Had she told me fifty shillings,
I might (and wouldn't you?)
Have referred to that dress in a way folks express
By an eloquent dash or two;
But the guileful little creature
Knew well her tactics when
She casually said that that dream in red
Had cost but two pounds ten.

Yet our home is all the brighter
For the dainty, sentient thing,
That floats away where it properly may,
And clings where it ought to cling;
And I count myself the luckiest
Of all us married men
That I have a wife whose joy in life
Is a gown at two pounds ten.

It isn't the gown compels me
Condone this venial sin;
It's the pretty face above the lace,

And the gentle heart within.

And with her arms about me

I say, and say again,

"'Twas wondrous cheap,"—and I think a heap

Of that gown at two pounds ten!

Eugene Field.

A PARAPHRASE

HOW happens it, my cruel miss,
You're always giving me the mitten?
You seem to have forgotten this:
That you no longer are a kitten!

A woman that has reached the years
Of that which people call discretion
Should put away all childish fears
And see in courtship no transgression.

A mother's solace may be sweet,
But Hymen's tenderness is sweeter;
And though all virile love be meet,
You'll find the poet's love is metre.

Eugene Field.

A LEAP-YEAR EPISODE

CAN I forget that winter night
In eighteen eighty-four,
When Nellie, charming little sprite,
Came tapping at the door?
"Good evening, miss," I blushing said,
For in my heart I knew—
And, knowing, hung my pretty head—
That Nellie came to woo.

She clasped my big red hand, and fell
Adown upon her knees,
And cried: "You know I love you well,
So be my husband, please!"
And then she swore she'd ever be
A tender wife and true—
Ah, what delight it was to me
That Nellie came to woo!

She'd lace my shoes and darn my hose
And mend my shirts, she said;
And grease my comely Roman nose
Each night on going to bed;
She'd build the fires and fetch the coal,
And split the kindling, too—
Love's perjuries o'erwhelmed her soul
When Nellie came to woo.

And as I blushing, gave no check
To her advances rash,
She twined her arms about my neck,

And toyed with my moustache;
And then she pleaded for a kiss,
While I—what could I do
But coyly yield me to that bliss
When Nellie came to woo?

I am engaged, and proudly wear
A gorgeous diamond ring,
And I shall wed my lover fair
Some time in gentle spring.
I face my doom without a sigh—
And so, forthsooth, would you,
If you but loved as fond as I
The Nellie who came to woo.

Eugene Field.

BALLADE OF LADIES' NAMES

BROWN'S for Lalage, Jones for Lelia,
Robinson's bosom for Beatrice glows,
Smith is a Hamlet before Ophelia.
The glamour stays if the reason goes!
Every lover the years disclose
Is of a beautiful name made free.
One befriends, and all others are foes.
Anna's the name of names for me.

Sentiment hallows the vowels of Delia;
Sweet simplicity breathes from Rose;
Courtly memories glitter in Celia;
Rosalind savours of quips and hose,
Araminta of wits and beaux,
Prue of puddings, and Coralie
All of sawdust and spangled shows;
Anna's the name of names for me.

Fie upon Caroline, Madge, Amelia—
These I reckon the essence of prose!—
Cavalier Katharine, cold Cornelia,
Portia's masterful Roman nose,

Maud's magnificence, Totty's toes,
Poll and Bet with their twang of the sea,
Nell's impertinence, Pamela's woes!
Anna's the name of names for me.

ENVOY

Ruth like a gillyflower smells and blows,

Sylvia prattles of Arcadee,
Sybil mystifies, Connie crows,
Anna's the name of names for me!

W. E. Henley.

BALLADE OF JUNE

LILACS glow, and jasmines climb,
Larks are loud the livelong day.
O the golden summer-prime!
June takes up the sceptre of May,
And the land beneath her sway
Glows, a dream of flowerful closes,
And the very wind's at play
With Sir Love among the roses.

Lights and shadows in the lime
Meet in exquisite disarray.
Hark! the rich recurrent rhyme
Of the blackbird's roundelay!
Where he carols, frank and gay,
Fancy no more glooms or proses;
Joyously she flits away
With Sir Love among the roses.

O the cool sea's slumbrous chime!
O the links that beach the bay,
Tricked with meadow-sweet and thyme,
Where the brown bees murmur and stray!
Lush the hedgerows, ripe the hay!
Many a maiden, binding posies,
Finds herself at Yea-and-Nay
With Sir Love among the roses.

ENVOY

Boys and girls, be wise, I pray!

Do as dear Queen June proposes,
For she bids you troop and stay
With Sir Love among the roses.
W. E. Henley.

BALLADE MADE IN THE HOT WEATHER

MOUNTAINS that frisk and sprinkle
The moss they overspill;
Grass that the breezes crinkle;
The wheel beside the mill,
With its wet, weedy frill;
Wind-shadows in the wheat;
A water-cart in the street;
The fringe of foam that girds
An islet's ferneries;
A green sky's minor thirds—
To live, I think of these!

Of ice and glass the tinkle,
Pellucid, silver-shrill;
Peaches without a wrinkle;
Cherries and snow, at will
From china bowls that fill
The senses with a sweet
Incuriousness of heat;
A melon's dripping sherds;
Cream-clotted strawberries;
Dusk dairies set with curds—
To live, I think of these!

Vale-lily and periwinkle;
Wet stone-crop on the sill;
The look of leaves a-twinkle
With windlets clear and still;
The feel of a forest rill

That wimples fresh and fleet
About one's naked feet;
The muzzles of drinking herds;
Lush flags and bulrushes;
The chirp of rain-bound birds—
To live, I think of these!

ENVOY

Dark aisles, new packs of cards,
Mermaidens' tails, cool swards,
Dawn dews and starlit seas,
White marbles, whiter words—
To live, I think of these!
W. E. Henley.

A ROSE

'TWAS a Jacqueminot rose
That she gave me at parting;
Sweetest flower that blows.
'Twas a Jacqueminot rose.
In the love garden close,
With the swift blushes starting,
'Twas a Jacqueminot rose
That she gave me at parting.

If she kissed it, who knows—
Since I will not discover,
And love is that close,
If she kissed it, who knows?
Or if not the red rose
Perhaps then the lover!
If she kissed it, who knows,
Since I will not discover.

Yet at least with the rose
Went a kiss that I'm wearing!
More I will not disclose,
Yet at least with the rose
Went whose kiss no one knows,—
Since I'm only declaring,
"Yet at least with the rose
Went a kiss that I'm wearing."

Arlo Bates.

TO MINNIE

(With a Hand Glass)

A PICTURE-FRAME for you to fill,
A paltry setting for your face,
A thing that has no worth until
You lend it something of your grace,

I send (unhappy I that sing
Laid by awhile upon the shelf)
Because I would not send a thing
Less charming than you are yourself.

And happier than I, alas!
(Dumb thing, I envy its delight)
'Twill wish you well, the looking-glass,
And look you in the face to-night.

Robert Louis Stevenson.

AN AMERICAN GIRL

SHE'S had a Vassar education,
And points with pride to her degrees;
She's studied household decoration:
She knows a dado from a frieze,
And tells Corots from Boldonis;
A Jacquemart etching, or a Haden,
A Whistler, too, perchance might please
A free and frank young Yankee maiden.

She does not care for meditation;
Within her bonnet are no bees;
She has a gentle animation,
She joins in singing simple glees.
She tries no trills, no rivalries
With Lucca (now Baronin Raden),
With Nilsson or with Gerster; she's
A free and frank young Yankee maiden.

I'm blessed above the whole creation,
Far, far, above all other he's;
I ask you for congratulation
On this the best of jubilees:
I go with her across the seas
Unto what Poe would call an Aiden,—
I hope no servant's there to tease
A free and frank young Yankee maiden.

ENVOY

Princes, to you the western breeze

Bears many a ship and heavy laden,
What is the best we send in these?
A free and frank young Yankee maiden.
Brander Matthews.

LARKS AND NIGHTINGALES

ALONE I sit at eventide:
The twilight glory pales,
And o'er the meadows far and wide
Chant pensive bobolinks.
(One might say nightingales!)

Song-sparrows warble on the tree,
I hear the purling brook,
And from the old "manse o'er the lea"
Flies slow the cawing crow.
(In England 'twere a rook!)

The last faint golden beams of day
Still glow on cottage panes,
And on their lingering homeward way
Walk weary laboring men.
(Oh, that we had swains!)

From farm-yards, down fair rural glades
Come sounds of tinkling bells,
And songs of merry brown milkmaids,
Sweeter than oriole's.
(Yes, thank you—Philomel's!)

I could sit here till morning came,
All through the night hours dark,
Until I saw the sun's bright flame
And heard the chickadee.
(Alas! we have no lark!)

We have no leas, no larks, no rooks,

No swains, no nightingales,
No singing milkmaids (save in books):
The poet does his best—
It is the rhyme that fails!

Nathan Haskell Dole.

CAELI

IF stars were really watching eyes
Of angel armies in the skies,
I should forget all watchers there,
And only for your glances care.

And if your eyes were really stars,
With leagues that none can mete for bars
To keep me from their longed-for day,
I could not feel more far away.

Francis William Bourdillon.

LADY MINE

LADY mine, most fair thou art
With youth's gold and white and red;
'Tis a pity that thy heart
Is so much harder than thy head.

This has stayed my kisses oft,
This from all thy charms debarr'd,
That thy head is strangely soft,
While thy heart is strangely hard.

Nothing had kept us apart—
I had loved thee, I had wed—
Hadst thou had a softer heart
Or a harder head.

But I think I'll bear Love's smart
Till the wound has healed and fled,
Or thy head is like thy heart,
Or thy heart is like thy head.

Herbert Edwin Clarke.

THE RIPEST PEACH[A]

THE ripest peach is highest on the tree—
And so her love, beyond the reach of me,
Is dearest in my sight. Sweet breezes, bow
Her heart down to me where I worship now!

She looms aloft where every eye may see
The ripest peach is highest on the tree.
Such fruitage as her love I know, alas!
I may not reach here from the orchard grass.

I drink the sunshine showered past her lips
As roses drain the dewdrop as it drips.
The ripest peach is highest on the tree,
And so mine eyes gaze upward eagerly.

Why—why do I not turn away in wrath
And pluck some heart here hanging in my path?—
Love's lower boughs bend with them—but, ah me!
The ripest peach is highest on the tree.

James Whitcomb Riley.

FOOTNOTES:

[A] From "Old-Fashioned Roses," copyright 1906. Used by special permission of the publishers, The Bobbs-Merrill Company.

"I JOURNEYED SOUTH TO MEET THE SPRING"

I JOURNEYED South to meet the Spring
To feel the soft tide's gentle rise
That to my heart again should bring,
Foretold by many a whispering wing,
The old, the new, the sweet surprise.

For once, the wonder was not new—
And yet it wore a newer grace:
For all its innocence of hue,
Its warmth and bloom and dream and dew,
I had but left—in Helen's face.

Robert Underwood Johnson.

BEFORE THE BLOSSOM

IN the tassel-time of spring
Love's the only song to sing;
Ere the ranks of solid shade
Hide the bluebird's flitting wing,
While in open forest glade
No mysterious sound or thing
Haunt of green has found or made,
Love's the only song to sing.

Though in May each bush be dressed
Like a bride, and every nest
Learn Love's joyous repetend,
Yet the half-told tale is best
At the budding,—with its end
Much too secret to be guessed,
And its fancies that attend
April's passion unexpressed.

Love and Nature communing
Gave us Arcady. Still ring—
Vales across and groves among—
Wistful memories, echoing
Pans far-off and fluty song
Poet! nothing harsher sing;
Be, like Love and Nature, young
In the tassel-time of spring.

Robert Underwood Johnson.

LOVE IN THE CALENDAR

WHEN chinks in April's windy dome
Let through a day of June,
And foot and thought incline to roam,
And every sound's a tune;
When Nature fills a fuller cup,
And hides with green the gray,—
Then, lover, pluck your courage up
To try your fate in May.

Though proud she was as sunset clad
In Autumn's fruity shades,
Love too is proud, and brings (gay lad!)
Humility to maids.
Scorn not from nature's mood to learn,
Take counsel of the day:
Since haughty skies to tender turn,
Go try your fate in May.

Though cold she seemed as pearly light
Adown December eves,
And stern as night when March winds smite
The beech's lingering leaves;
Yet Love hath seasons like the year,
And grave will turn to gay,—
Then, lover, hearken not to fear,
But try your fate in May.

And you whose art it is to hide
The constant love you feel:
Beware, lest overmuch of pride

Your happiness shall steal.
No longer pout, for May is here,
And hearts will have their way;
Love's in the calendar, my dear,
So yield to fate—and May!

Robert Underwood Johnson.

MY GRANDMOTHER'S TURKEY-TAIL FAN

IT owned not a color that vanity dons
Or slender wits choose for display;
Its beautiful tint was a delicate bronze,
A brown softly blended with gray.
From her waist to her chin, spreading out without break,
'Twas built on a generous plan:
The pride of the forest was slaughtered to make
My grandmother's turkey-tail fan.

For common occasions it never was meant:
In a chest between two silken cloths
'Twas kept safely hidden with careful intent
In camphor to keep out the moths.
'Twas famed far and wide through the whole country side,
From Beersheba e'en unto Dan;
And often at meeting with envy 'twas eyed,
My grandmother's turkey-tail fan.

Camp-meetings, indeed, were its chiefest delight.
Like a crook unto sheep gone astray
It beckoned backsliders to re-seek the right,
And exhorted the sinners to pray.
It always beat time when the choir went wrong,
In psalmody leading the van.
Old Hundred, I know, was its favorite song—
My grandmother's turkey-tail fan.

A fig for the fans that are made nowadays,
Suited only to frivolous mirth!
A different thing was the fan that I praise,

Yet it scorned not the good things of earth.
At bees and at quiltings 'twas aye to be seen;
The best of the gossip began
When in at the doorway had entered serene
My grandmother's turkey-tail fan.

Tradition relates of it wonderful tales.
Its handle of leather was buff.
Though shorn of its glory, e'en now it exhales
An odor of hymn-books and snuff.
Its primeval grace, if you like, you can trace:
'Twas limned for the future to scan,
Just under a smiling gold-spectacled face,
My grandmother's turkey-tail fan.

Samuel Minturn Peck.

VALENTINE

IF thou canst make the frost be gone,
And fleet away the snow
(And that thou canst, I trow);
If thou canst make the spring to dawn,
Hawthorn to put her brav'ry on,
Willow, her weeds of fine green lawn,
Say why thou dost not so—
Aye, aye!
Say why
Thou dost not so!

If thou canst chase the stormy rack,
And bid the soft winds blow
(And that thou canst, I trow);
If thou canst call the thrushes back
To give the groves the songs they lack,
And wake the violet in thy track,
Say why thou dost not so—
Aye, aye!
Say why
Thou dost not so!

If thou canst make my winter spring,
With one word breathed low
(And that thou canst, I know);
If in the closure of a ring
Thou canst to me such treasure bring,
My state shall be above a king,
Say why thou dost not so—

Aye, aye!

Say why

Thou dost not so!

Edith Matilda Thomas.

A VALENTINE

OH! little loveliest lady mine,
What shall I send for your valentine?
Summer and flowers are far away;
Gloomy old Winter is king to-day;
Buds will not blow, and sun will not shine:
What shall I do for a valentine?

I've searched the gardens all through and through
For a bud to tell of my love so true;
But buds are asleep, and blossoms are dead,
And the snow beats down on my poor little head:
So, little loveliest lady mine,
Here is my heart for your valentine!

Laura Elizabeth Richards.

ON A HYMN-BOOK

OLD hymn-book, sure I thought I'd lost you
In the days now long gone by;
I'd forgotten where I tossed you:
Gracious! how I sigh.

In the church a thin partition
Stood between her pew and mine;
And her pious, sweet contrition
Struck me as divine.

Yes, remarkably entrancing
Was she in her sable furs;
And my eyes were always glancing
Up, old book, to hers.

Bless you, very well she knew it,
And I'm sure she liked it too;
Once she whispered, "Please don't do it,"
But her eyes said, "Do."

How to speak—to tell my passion?
How to make her think me true?
Love soon found a curious fashion,
For he spoke through you.

How I used to search your pages
For the words I wished to say;
And received my labour's wages
Every Sabbath day.

Ah, how sweet it was to hand her
You, with lines I'd marked when found!

And how well I'd understand her
When she blushed and frowned.

And one day, old book, you wriggled
From my hand and, rattling fell
Upon the floor; and she—she giggled,
Did Miss Isabel.

Then when next we met out walking,
I was told in fearful tones,
How she'd got a dreadful talking
From the Reverend Jones.

Ah me! No man could resist her
In those sweet and buried years,
So I think—I think I kissed her,
Just to stop her tears.

Jones I gave a good sound chaffing;
Called his sermon dry as bones;
Soon fair Isabel was laughing—
Said she hated Jones.

It was after that I lost you,
For I needed you no more;
Somewhere—anywhere I tossed you
On a closet floor.

Reverend Samuel still preaches;
Isabel her past atones;
In his Sunday-school she teaches—
Mrs. Samuel Jones.

W. J. Henderson.

THE BALLADE OF THE SUMMER-BOARDER

*L*ET *all men living on earth take heed,*
For their own soul's sake, to a rhyme well meant;
Writ so that he who runs may read—
We are the folk that a-summering went,
Who while the year was young were bent—
Yea, bent on doing this self-same thing
Which we have done unto some extent.
This is the end of our summering.

We are the folk who would fain be freed
From wasteful burdens of rate and rent—
From the vampire agents' ravening breed—
We are the folk that a-summering went.
We hied us forth when the summer was blent
With the fresh faint sweetness of dying spring,
A-seeking the meadows dew besprent
This is the end of our summering.

For O the waiters that must be fee'd,
And our meat-time neighbour, the travelling "gent";
And the youth next door with the ophicleide!
We are the folk that a-summering went!
Who from small bare rooms wherein we were pent,
While birds their way to the southward wing,
Come back, our money for no good spent—
This is the end of our summering.

ENVOY

Citizens! list to our sore lament—

While the landlord's hands to our raiment cling—
We are the folk that a-summering went:
This is the end of our summering.

H. C. Bunner.

INTERESTING

I ROWED her out on the broad bright sea,
Till the land lay purple upon our lee.

The heavens were trying the waves to outshine,
With never a cloud to the far sea-line.

On the reefs the billows in kisses broke—
But oh, I was dying for one small smoke.

She spoke of the gulls and the waters green—
But what is nature to Nicotine?

She spoke of the tides, and the Triton myth;
And said Jones was engaged to the blonde Miss Smith.

She spoke of her liking lemon on clams;
And Euclid, and parallelograms.

For her face was fair and her eyes were brown,
And she was a girl from Boston town.

And I rowed and thought—but I never said—
"Does Havana tobacco trouble your head?"

She talked of algæ—she talked of sand—
And I thought: "Tobacco you cannot stand."

She talked of the ocean-steamer's speed—
And I yearned for a whiff of the wicked weed.

And at last I spoke, between fright and fret:
"Would you mind if I smoked a cigarette?"

She dropped her eyes on the ocean's blue,
And said: "Would you mind if I smoked too?"

H. C. Bunner.

THE WAY TO ARCADY

OH, what's the way to Arcady,
To Arcady, to Arcady;
Oh, what's the way to Arcady,
Where all the leaves are merry?

Oh, what's the way to Arcady?
The spring is rustling in the tree—
The tree the wind is blowing through—
It sets the blossoms flickering white.
I knew not skies could burn so blue
Nor any breezes blow so light.
They blow an old-time way for me,
Across the world to Arcady.

Oh, what's the way to Arcady?
Sir Poet, with the rusty coat,
Quit mocking of the song-bird's note.
How have you heart for any tune,
You with the wayworn russet shoon?
Your scrip, a-swinging by your side,
Gapes with a gaunt mouth hungry-wide.
I'll brim it well with pieces red,
If you will tell the way to tread.

Oh, I am bound for Arcady,
And if you but keep pace with me
You tread the way to Arcady.

And where away lies Arcady,
And how long yet may the journey be?

Ah, that (quoth he) I do not know—
Across the clover and the snow—
Across the frost, across the flowers—
Through summer seconds and winter hours.
I've trod the way my whole life long,
And know not now where it may be;
My guide is but the stir to song,
That tells me I cannot go wrong,
Or clear or dark the pathway be
Upon the road to Arcady.

But how shall I do who cannot sing?
I was wont to sing, once on a time—
There is never an echo now to ring
Remembrance back to the trick of rhyme.

'Tis strange you cannot sing (quoth he),
The folk all sing in Arcady.

But how may he find Arcady
Who hath nor youth nor melody?

What, know you not, old man (quoth he)—
Your hair is white, your face is wise—
That Love must kiss that Mortal's eyes
Who hopes to see fair Arcady?
No gold can buy you entrance there;
But beggared Love may go all bare—
No wisdom won with weariness;
But Love goes in with Folly's dress—
No fame that wit could ever win;
But only Love may lead Love in

To Arcady, to Arcady.

Ah, woe is me, through all my days
Wisdom and wealth I both have got,
And fame and name, and great men's praise,
But Love, ah, Love! I have it not.
There was a time, when life was new—
But far away, and half forgot—
I only know her eyes were blue;
But Love—I fear I knew it not.
We did not wed, for lack of gold,
And she is dead, and I am old.
All things have come since then to me,
Save Love, ah, Love! and Arcady.

Ah, then I fear we part (quoth he),
My way's for Love and Arcady.

But you, you fare alone, like me;
The gray is likewise in your hair.
What love have you to lead you there,
To Arcady, to Arcady?

Ah, no, not lonely do I fare;
My true companion's Memory.
With Love he fills the Spring-time air;
With Love he clothes the Winter tree.
Oh, past this poor horizon's bound
My song goes straight to one who stands—
Her face all gladdening at the sound—
To lead me to the Spring-green lands,
To wander with enlacing hands.

The songs within my breast that stir
Are all of her, are all of her.
My maid is dead long years (quoth he),
She waits for me in Arcady.

Oh, yon's the way to Arcady,
To Arcady, to Arcady;
Oh, yon's the way to Arcady,
Where all the leaves are merry.

H. C. Bunner.

DA CAPO

SHORT and sweet, and we've come to the end of it—
Our poor little love lying cold.
Shall no sonnet, then, ever be penned of it?
Nor the joys and pains of it told?
How fair was its face in the morning,
How close its caresses at noon,
How its evening grew chill without warning,
Unpleasantly soon!

I can't say just how we began it—
In a blush, or a smile, or a sigh;
Fate took but an instant to plan it;
It needs but a moment to die.
Yet—remember that first conversation,
When the flowers you had dropped at your feet
I restored. The familiar quotation
Was—"Sweets to the sweet."

Oh, their delicate perfume has haunted
My senses a whole season through.
If there was one soft charm that you wanted
The violets lent it to you.
I whispered you, life was but lonely:
A cue which you graciously took;
And your eyes learned a look for me only—
A very nice look.

And sometimes your hand would touch my hand,
With a sweetly particular touch;
You said many things in a sigh, and

Made a look express wondrously much.
We smiled for the mere sake of smiling,
And laughed for no reason but fun;
Irrational joys; but beguiling—
And all that is done!

We were idle, and played for a moment
At a game that now neither will press:
I cared not to find out what "No" meant;
Nor your lips to grow yielding with "Yes."
Love is done with and dead; if there lingers
A faint and indefinite ghost,
It is laid with this kiss on your fingers—
A jest at the most.

'Tis a commonplace, stale situation,
Now the curtain comes down from above
On the end of our little flirtation—
A travesty romance for Love,
If he climbed in disguise to your lattice,
Fell dead of the first kisses' pain:
But one thing is left us now; that is—
Begin it again.

H. C. Bunner.

THE MAID OF MURRAY HILL

SAINT Valentine, Saint Valentine!
I love a maid of New York town,
And every day, on my homeward way,
She walks the Avenue down.
At five o'clock, dear Saint, she goes
Tripping down Murray Hill,
And the hands of the clock in the old brick spire
Stand still, stand still, stand still!

Saint Valentine, Saint Valentine!
Oh, could you know how fair a maid—
So trim of dress, and so gold of tress,
You'd know why I'm afraid.
I see her pass, I smile and bow,
As I go up Murray Hill,
And I say to a foolish hope of mine:
Be still, be still, be still!

Saint Valentine, Saint Valentine,
Oh, could you see how close her gown
Binds tight and warm about her form,
This maid of New York town,
You'd know a mountain would to me
Be less than Murray Hill,
If only around her my arm could slip,
And she'd stand still, stand still.

Saint Valentine, Saint Valentine!
She is so fair, so rich, so great,
I have no right to think what might

Be this poor clerk's estate.

And yet the bells in yon brick spire,

As we pass on Murray Hill,

They ring, they ring—she's not for me—

And still—and still—and still—

H. C. Bunner.

KITTY'S SUMMERING

HAVE you seen e'er a sign of my Kitty?
Have you seen a fair maiden go by
Who was wed in this summer-struck city
About the first week in July?
How fair was her face there's no telling;
She was well-nigh as wealthy as fair,
And of marble and brick was her dwelling
On the North side of Washington Square.

Have you seen her at Newport a-driving?
Have you seen her a-flirt at the pier?
Is she written among the arriving
At the Shoals or the Hamptons this year?
Or out where the ocean bird flutters
Are the sea-breezes tossing her hair?
For closed are the ancient green shutters
In the house on North Washington Square.

So you, too, are trying to find her?
Then climb up these stairways with me,
That twist and grow blinder and blinder,
Till the skylight near heaven you see.
Is the sun my dull studio gilding?
Ah, no, it is Kitty sits there—
She has moved to the Studio Building
On the South side of Washington Square.

H. C. Bunner.

FORFEITS

THEY sent him round the circle fair,
To bow before the prettiest there.
I'm bound to say the choice he made
A creditable taste displayed;
Although—I can't say what it meant—
The little maid looked ill-content.

His task was then anew begun—
To kneel before the wittiest one.
Once more that little maid sought he,
And went him down upon his knee.
She bent her eyes upon the floor—
I think she thought the game a bore.

He circled then—his sweet behest
To kiss the one he loved the best.
For all she frowned, for all she chid,
He kissed that little maid, he did.
And then—though why I can't decide—
The little maid looked satisfied.

H. C. Bunner.

WHEN WILL LOVE COME?

SOME find Love late, some find him soon,
Some with the rose in May,
Some with the nightingale in June,
And some when skies are grey;
Love comes to some with smiling eyes,
And comes with tears to some;
For some Love sings, for some Love sighs,
For some Love's lips are dumb.
How will you come to me, fair Love?
Will you come late or soon?
With sad or smiling skies above,
By light of sun or moon?
Will you be sad, will you be sweet,
Sing, sigh, Love, or be dumb?
Will it be summer when we meet,
Or autumn ere you come?

Pakenham Beatty.

HELIOTROPE

AMID the Chapel's chequered gloom
She laughed with Dora and with Flora
And chattered in the lecture-room—
That saucy little sophomora!
Yet while, as in her other schools,
She was a privileged transgressor,
She never broke the simple rules
Of one particular professor.

But when he spoke of varied lore,
Paroxytones and modes potential,
She listened with a face that wore
A look half fond, half reverential.
To her, that earnest voice was sweet,
And, though her love had no confessor,
Her girlish heart lay at the feet
Of that particular professor.

And he had learned, among his books
That held the lore of ages olden,
To watch those ever-changing looks,
The wistful eyes, the tresses golden,
That stirred his pulse with passion's pain
And thrilled his soul with soft desire,
And bade fond youth return again,
Crowned with its coronet of fire.

Her sunny smile, her winsome ways,
Were more to him than all his knowledge,
And she preferred his words of praise

To all the honours of the college.
Yet "What am foolish I to him?"
She whispered to her heart's confessor.
"She thinks me old and grey and grim,"
In silence pondered the professor.

Yet once when Christmas bells were rung
Above ten thousand solemn churches,
And swelling anthems grandly sung
Pealed through the dim cathedral arches;
Ere home returning, filled with hope,
Softly she stole by gate and gable,
And a sweet spray of heliotrope
Left on his littered study table.

Nor came she more from day to day
Like sunshine through the shadows rifting:
Above her grave, far, far away,
The ever silent snows were drifting;
And those who mourned her winsome face
Found in its stead a sweet successor
And loved another in her place—
All, save the silent old professor.

But, in the tender twilight grey,
Shut from the sight of carping critic,
His lonely thoughts would often stray
From Vedic verse and tongues Semitic,
Bidding the ghost of vanished hope
Mock with its past the sad possessor
Of the dead spray of heliotrope

That once she gave the old professor.

Harry Thurston Peck.

BORDERLAND

AND have you been to Borderland?
Its country lies on either hand
Beyond the river I-forget.
One crosses by a single stone
So narrow one must pass alone,
And all about its waters fret—
The laughing river I-forget.

Beneath the trees of Borderland
One seems to know and understand,
Beside the river I-forget,
All languages of men and birds;
And all the sweet, unspoken words
One ever missed are murmured yet
By that sweet river I-forget.

One hears there many things afar
From cities where strange peoples are,
Beyond the river I-forget;
And stranger things are in the air,
But what they are one does not care,
For Hope lies sleeping and Regret
Beside the river I-forget.

Some day together hand in hand
I'll take you there to Borderland,
Beyond the river I-forget;
Some day when all our dreams come true,
One kiss for me and one for you,
We'll watch the red sun sink and set

Across the river I-forget.

Herman Knickerbocker Vielé.

EPITHALAMIUM

THE marriage bells have rung their peal,
The wedding march has told its story.
I've seen her at the altar kneel
In all her stainless, virgin glory;
She's bound to honor, love, obey,
Come joy or sorrow, tears or laughter.
I watched her as she rode away,
And flung the lucky slipper after.

She was my first, my very first,
My earliest inamorata,
And to the passion that I nursed
For her I well nigh was a martyr.
For I was young, and she was fair,
And always gay and bright and chipper,
And, oh, she wore such sunlit hair,
Such silken stockings! such a slipper!

She did not wish to make me mourn—
She was the kindest of God's creatures;
But flirting was in her inborn,
Like brains and queerness in the Beechers.
I do not fear your heartless flirt—
Obtuse her dart and dull her probe is;
But when girls do not mean to hurt,
But *do—Orate tunc pro nobis!*

A most romantic country place;
The moon at full, the month of August;
An inland lake across whose face

Played gentle zephyrs, ne'er a raw gust.
Books, boats, and horses to enjoy,
The which was all our occupation;
A damsel and a callow boy—
There! now you have the situation.

We rode together miles and miles,
My pupil she, and I her Chiron;
At home I reveled in her smiles
And read her extracts out of Byron.
We roamed by moonlight, chose our stars
(I thought it most authentic billing),
Explored the woods, climbed over bars,
Smoked cigarettes and broke a shilling.

An infinitely blissful week
Went by in this Arcadian fashion;
I hesitated long to speak,
But ultimately breathed my passion.
She said her heart was not her own;
She said she'd love me like a sister;
She cried a little (not alone);
I begged her not to fret, and—kissed her.

I lost some sleep, some pounds in weight,
A deal of time, and all my spirits,
And much—how much I dare not state—
I mused upon that damsel's merits.
I tortured my unhappy soul,
I wished I never might recover;
I hoped her marriage bells might toll

A requiem for her faithful lover.

And now she's married, now she wears
A wedding-ring upon her finger;
And I—although it odd appears—
Still in the flesh I seem to linger.
Lo, there my swallow-tail, and here
Lies by my side a wedding favor;
Beside it stands a mug of beer,
I taste it—how divine its flavor!

I saw her in her bridal dress
Stand pure and lovely at the altar;
I heard her firm response—that "Yes,"
Without a quiver or a falter.
And here I sit and drink to her
Long life and happiness, God bless her!
Now fill again. No heel-taps, sir;
Here's to—Success to her successor!

E. S. Martin.

INFIRM

"I WILL not go," he said, "for well
I know her eyes' insidious spell,
And how unspeakably he feels
Who takes no pleasure in his meals.
I know a one-idea'd man
Should undergo the social ban,
And if she once my purpose melts
I know I'll think of nothing else.

"I care not though her teeth are pearls—
The town is full of nicer girls!
I care not though her lips are red—
It does not do to lose one's head!
I'll give her leisure to discover,
For once, how little I think of her;
And then, how will she feel?" cried he—
And took his hat and went to see.

E. S. Martin.

WORDS, WORDS, WORDS

I LOVED a maid (oh, she was fair of face!)
But common words above
Was my true love—
So I was silent for a little space—
Yet, 'gainst the day I meant that she should hear me,
I sought for stately words that might endear me.

My ardent lips, I vowed, should not repeat
What countless lovers swear:—
"Oh, thou art fair!"
I scorned to merely say, "I love thee, Sweet!"
So spent long days with rhetoric and tutor,
In framing sentences I dreamed might suit her.

Oh, how I pondered what she best might hear!
Words should like jewels shine
To make her mine—
No commonplaces must offend her ear:
But while for proper words my passion tarried
I learned the maiden some one else had married!

Margaret Deland.

THE BLUEBELL

IN love she fell,
My shy Bluebell,
With a strolling Bumblebee;
"I love you so,"
He whispered low,
"Sweet, give your heart to me!"

"I love but you,
And I'll be true,
Oh, give me your heart, I pray?"
She bent her head,—
"I will," she said;
When, lo, he flew away!

Margaret Deland.

A MODERN MARTYRDOM

THE Weverwend Awthur Murway Gween,
They say is verwy clevah;
And sister Wuth could heah him pweach,
Fohevah and fohevah.
And I went down to heah him pweach,
With Wuth and my Annette,
Upon the bwave, hewoic deaths
The ancient mawtahs met;
And as he wepwesented them,
In all their acts and feachaws,
The ancient mawtahs, dontcherknow?
Were doocid clevah cweachaws.

But, aw deah me! They don't compah
In twue hewoic bwavewy,
To a bwave hewo fwiend of mine,
Young Montmowenci Averwy.
He earned foah dollahs everwy week,
And not anothah coppah;
But this bwave soul wesolved to dwess
Pwe-eminently pwoppah.
So this was all the food each day,
The bwave young cweachaw had—
One glaws of milk, a cigawette,
Foah cwackers, and some bwead.

He lived on foahteen cents a day,
And cherwished one great passion:
The pwecious pwoject of his soul,

Of being dwessed in fashion.
But when he'd earned a suit entiah,
To his supweme chagwin,
Just then did shawt-tailed coats go out,
And long-tailed coats come in;
But naught could bweak his wigid will
And now, I pway you, note,
That he gave up his glaws of milk
And bought a long-tailed coat.

But then the fashion changed once moah,
And bwought a gwievous plight;
It changed from twousers that are loose
To twousers that are tight.
Then his foah cwackers he gave up,
He just wenounced their use;
And changed to twousers that are tight
From twousers that are loose.
And then the narrow-toed style shoes
To bwoad-toed changed instead;
Then he pwocured a bwoad-toed paih,
And gave up eating bwead.

Just then the bwoad-bwimmed style of hat
To narrow bwims gave way;
And so his twibulations gwew,
Incweasing everwy day.
But he pwocured a narrow bwim,
Of verwy stylish set;
But bwave, bwave soul! he had to dwop
His pwecious cigawette.

But now when his whole suit confohmed
To fashion's wegulation
For lack of cwackers, milk, and bwead,
He perwished of stahvation.

Thus in his owah of victowry,
He passed on to his west—
I weally nevah saw a cawpse
So fashionably dwessed.
My teahs above his well-dwessed clay
Fell like the spwingtime wains;
My eyes had nevah wested on
Such pwoppah dwessed wemains.
The ancient mawtahs—they were gwand
And glowious in their day;
But this bwave Montmowenci was
As gweat and gwand as they.

Sam Walter Foss.

A CORSAGE BOUQUET

M<small>YRTILLA</small>, to-night,

Wears Jacqueminot roses,

She's the loveliest sight!

Myrtilla to-night:—

Correspondingly light

My pocket-book closes.

Myrtilla, to-night

Wears Jacqueminot roses.

Charles Henry Lüders.

THE BALLAD OF CASSANDRA BROWN

THOUGH I met her in the summer, when one's heart lies 'round at ease

As it were in tennis costume, and a man's not hard to please;

Yet I think at any season to have met her was to love,

While her tones, unspoiled, unstudied, had the softness of the dove.

At request she read us poems, in a nook among the pines,

And her artless voice lent music to the least melodious lines;

Though she lowered her shadowing lashes, in an earnest reader's wise,

Yet we caught blue gracious glimpses of the heavens that were her eyes.

As in Paradise I listened. Ah, I did not understand

That a little cloud, no larger than the average human hand,

Might, as stated oft in fiction, spread into a sable pall,

When she said that she should study elocution in the fall.

I admit her earliest efforts were not in the Ercles vein:

She began with "Lit-tle Maaybel, with her faayce against the paayne,

And the beacon-light a-trrremble—" which, although it made me wince,

Is a thing of cheerful nature to the things she's rendered since.

Having learned the Soulful Quiver, she acquired the Melting Mo-o-an,

And the way she gave "Young Grayhead" would have liquefied a stone;

Then the Sanguinary Tragic did her energies employ,

And she tore my taste to tatters when she slew "The Polish Boy."

It's not pleasant for a fellow when the jewel of his soul

Wades through slaughter on the carpet, while her orbs in frenzy roll:

What was I that I should murmur? Yet it gave me grievous pain,

When she rose in social gatherings and "searched among the slain."

I was forced to look upon her, in my desperation dumb—
Knowing well that when her awful opportunity was come
She would give us battle, murder, sudden death at very least—
As a skeleton of warning, and a blight upon the feast.

Once, ah! once I fell a-dreaming; some one played a polonaise
I associated strongly with those happier August days;
And I mused, "I'll speak this evening," recent pangs forgotten quite.
Sudden shrilled a scream of anguish: "Curfew SHALL not ring to-night!"

Ah, that sound was as a curfew, quenching rosy warm romance!
Were it safe to wed a woman one so oft would wish in France?
Oh, as she "cull-imbed" that ladder, swift my mounting hope came down.
I am still a single cynic; she is still Cassandra Brown!

Helen Gray Cone.

FROM THREE FLY LEAVES

AH Phyllis! did I only dare
To hope that, as the years go by,
And you, a maid divinely fair,
The cynosure of every eye,
Have fixed the wandering minds of men,
And found a fare for scores of hearses,
You still will open, now and then,
My little book of verses;

Or did I, bolder yet, aspire
To hope that any phrase of mine,
Aglow with memory's cheering fire
Will burn within that heart of thine;
Although my brow be bare of bays,
My coffers not replete with gain,
I shall not—what's the foolish phrase?—
Have written quite in vain.

J. K. Stephen.

QUESTION AND ANSWER

THE QUESTION

THE river is flowing,
The stars coming forth:
Great ruddy clouds going
From westward to north.

The rushes are waving,
The water's still blue:
And I am behaving
Decorously too:

The amorous zephyr
Breathes soft in our ear:
Who hears not is deafer
Than adders, my dear:

Ah! list to the whisper
Of waters and sky!
Thames, vagabond lisper
Grows subtle and sly.

How trebly delicious
The air-draughts we quaff:
The hour is propitious:—
Oh! . . . why do you laugh?

THE ANSWER

Ask the sky why it flushes,
The clouds why they glow:
The weir why it gushes,

The reeds why they grow:

The moon why it rises,
The sun why it sets:
Her why she surprises,
Him why he forgets:

The star why it twinkles,
The west why it shines:
The brow why it wrinkles,
The heart why it pines:

Mankind why they blunder,
The corn why there's chaff:
Ask yourself why you wonder—
Not me why I laugh!

J. K. Stephen.

A RHYME FOR PRISCILLA

DEAR Priscilla, quaint and very
Like a modern Puritan,
Is a modest, literary,
Merry young American:
Horace she has read, and Bion
Is her favorite in Greek;
Shakespeare is a mighty lion
In whose den she dares but peek;
Him she leaves to some sage Daniel,
Since of lions she's afraid,—
She prefers a playful spaniel,
Such as Herrick or as Praed;
And it's not a bit satiric
To confess her fancy goes
From the epic to a lyric
On a rose.

Wise Priscilla, dilettante,
With a sentimental mind,
Doesn't deign to dip in Dante
And to Milton isn't kind;
L'Allegro, Il Penseroso
Have some merits she will grant,
All the rest is only so-so,—
Enter Paradise she can't!
She might make a charming angel
(And she will if she is good),
But it's doubtful if the change'll

Make the Epic understood:
Honey-suckling, like a bee she
Goes and pillages his sweets,
And it's plain enough to see she
Worships Keats.

Gay Priscilla,—just the person
For the Locker whom she loves;
What a captivating verse on
Her neat-fitting gowns or gloves
He could write in catching measure,
Setting all the heart astir!
And to Aldrich what a pleasure
It would be to sing of her,—
He, whose perfect songs have won her
Lips to quote them day by day.
She repeats the rhymes of Bunner
In a fascinating way,
And you'll often find her lost in—
She has reveries at times—
Some delightful one of Austin
Dobson's rhymes.

O Priscilla, sweet Priscilla,
Writing of you makes me think,
As I burn my brown Manila
And immortalize my ink,
How well satisfied these poets
Ought to be with what they do
When, especially, they know it's
Read by such a girl as you:

I who sing of you would marry
Just the kind of girl you are,—
One who doesn't care to carry
Her poetic taste too far,—
One whose fancy is a bright one,
Who is fond of poems fine,
And appreciates a light one
Such as mine.

Frank Dempster Sherman.

THE OLD COLLECTOR

'TIS strange to look across the street
And feel that we no more shall greet
Our middle-aged, precise, and neat,
Old-fashioned neighbor.
It seems, in his unlighted hall,
His much-prized pictures on the wall
Must miss his presence, and recall
His loving labor.

His manner was serene and fine,
Fashioned on some Old-World design.
His wit grew keener with the wine,
And kindlier after;
And when the revelry rang high,
No one could make more apt reply;
Yet, though they sometimes marked his sigh,
None heard his laughter.

He held as foolish him who dotes
On politics or petticoats;
He vowed he'd hear no talk of votes
Or silly scandals.
No journeys tempted him; he swore
He held his world within his door,
And there he'd dwell till life was o'er,
Secure from vandals.

"Why should I roam the world again?"
He said. "Domingo shows me Spain;
The dust of travel then were vain.

What springtime chances
To match my Corot there! One glance
Is worth a year of actual France.
The real ne'er equals the romance,
Nor fact our fancies."

His walls were decked with maidens fair—
A Henner with rich auburn hair;
A Reynolds with the stately air
That fits a beauty;
There glanced a Greuze with girlish grace;
And yonder, with the strong, calm face,
The peasant sister of her race,
Whose life is duty.

He valued most the sunny day
Because it lighted his Dupré,
And showed his small Meissonier
In proper fashion.
And tender was the glance he bent
Upon his missal's ornament,
Whereon some patient monk had spent
His artist passion.

I used to love to see him pass
His fingers o'er some rare old glass.
He never took delight *en masse;*
He loved each treasure:
The precious bronzes from Japan,
The rugs from towered Ispahan,
His rose-tint Sèvres, his famous fan—

Each had its pleasure.

And so he held that Art was all;
Yet when Death made the solemn call,
Before the desk in his long hall
They found him sitting.
Within the hands clasped on his breast
An old daguerreotype was pressed—
A sweet-faced, smiling girl, and dressed
In frills befitting.

Naught of his story can we know,
Nor whose the fault so long ago,
Nor with what meed of weal or woe
His love was blended.
Yet o'er his rare Delft mantel-tiles
Bellini's sweet Madonna smiles
As though she knew the weary miles
For him are ended.

Beatrice Hanscom.

THE LAST DITCH

LOVE, through your varied views on Art
Untiring have I followed you,
Content to know I had your heart
And was your Art-ideal, too.

As, dear, I was when first we met.
('Twas at the time you worshipped Leighton,
And were attempting to forget
Your Foster and your Noel Paton.)

"Love rhymes with Art," said your dear voice,
And, at my crude, uncultured age,
I could but blushingly rejoice
That you had passed the Rubens stage.

When Madox Brown and Morris swayed
Your taste, did I not dress and look
Like any Middle Ages maid
In an illuminated book?

I wore strange garments, without shame,
Of formless form and toneless tones,
I might have stepped out of the frame
Of a Rossetti or Burne-Jones.

I stole soft frills from Marcus Stone,
My waist wore Herkomer's disguise,
My slender purse was strained, I own,
But—my silk lay as Sargent's lies.

And when you were abroad—in Prague—
'Mid Cherets I had shone, a star;

Then for your sake I grew as vague
As Mr. Whistler's ladies are.

But now at last you sue in vain,
For here a life's submission ends:
Not even for you will I grow plain
As Aubrey Beardsley's "lady friends."

Here I renounce your hand—unless
You find your Art-ideal elsewhere;
I *will not* wear the kind of dress
That Laurence Housman's people wear!

E. Nesbit.

BE YE IN LOVE WITH APRIL-TIDE

BE ye in love with April-tide?

I' faith, in love am I!

For now 'tis sun, and now 'tis shower,

And now 'tis frost, and now 'tis flower,

And now 'tis Laura laughing-eyed,

And now 'tis Laura shy!

Ye doubtful days, O slower glide!

Still smile and frown, O sky!

Some beauty unforeseen I trace

In every change of Laura's face;—

Be ye in love with April-tide?

I' faith, in love am I!

Clinton Scollard.

STRAWBERRIES

AGAIN the year is at the prime
With flush of rose and cuckoo-croon;
Care doffs his wrinkled air, and Time
Foots to a gamesome tune.
So, ho, my lads, an' if you will
But follow underneath the hill,
It's strawberries! strawberries!
You shall feast, and have your fill!

The elder clusters promise wine
Where dips the path along the lane;
The early lowing of the kine
Floats in a far refrain;
You will forget to dream indeed
Of fruit that Georgian loam-lands breed
In strawberries! strawberries!
That wait for us in Martin's mead.

Then haste, before the sun be high,
And, haply, catch the morning star;
For, ere the cups of dew be dry,
The berries sweetest are.
And if, perchance, a rustic lass
In merriment a-milking pass,
It's strawberries! strawberries!
On her lips as in the grass.

Clinton Scollard.

APPLIED ASTRONOMY

HE took me out to see the stars,
That astronomic bore;
He said there were two moons near Mars,
While Jupiter had four.

I thought of course he'd whisper soon
What fourfold bliss 'twould be
To stroll beneath that fourfold moon
On Jupiter with me.

And when he spoke of Saturn's ring,
I was convinced he'd say
That was the very kind of thing
To offer me some day.

But in a tangent off he went
To double stars. Now that
Was most suggestive, so content
And quite absorbed I sat.

But no, he talked a dreary mess,
Of which the only fraction
That caught my fancy, I confess,
Was "mutual attraction."

I said I thought it very queer
And stupid altogether,
For stars to keep so very near,
And yet not come together.

At that he smiled, and turned his head;
I thought he'd caught the notion.

He merely bowed good-night and said,
Their safety lay in motion.

Esther B. Tiffany.

COURTSHIP

IT chanced, they say, upon a day,
A furlong from the town,
That she was strolling up the way
As he was strolling down—
She humming low, as might be so,
A ditty sweet and small;
He whistling loud a tune, you know,
That had no tune at all.
It happened so—precisely so—
As all their friends and neighbours know.

As I and you perhaps might do,
They gazed upon the ground;
But when they'd gone a yard or two
Of course they both looked round.
They both were pained, they both explained
What caused their eyes to roam;
And nothing after that remained
But he should see her home.
It happened so—precisely so
As all their friends and neighbours know.

Next day to that 'twas common chat,
Admitting no debate,
A bonnet close beside a hat
Was sitting on a gate.
A month, not more, had bustled o'er,
When, braving nod and smile,
One blushing soul came through the door

Where two went up the aisle.

It happened so—precisely so—

As all their friends and neighbours know.

Frederick Langbridge.

EYES OF BLACK AND EYES OF BLUE

(From the Viceroy)

ONE day I swear by the eyes of black,
The next by the eyes of blue;
'Tis in merry black eyes that the love-light lies,
But the blue are more apt to be true.
The dusky-eyed maid has a laughing look
That can make you the world forget, my boy;
But the gentle blue eye never causes a sigh,
And it rarely denotes the coquette, my boy.

Eyes of black or eyes of blue,
Devil a bit does it matter I say!
If I love one to-day, why to-morrow I may
Have a caprice for the brown or the gray.
So here is a toast to the feminine host,
The blue eyes for me or the black for you.
The one for a time I shall think sublime,
And then if you like I will change with you.

One day I sing of the raven curls,
The next of the ringlets fair.
Be mine the brunette of the tresses jet,
Mine the Hebe of golden hair.
For the gypsy-like maid has a heart that's warm,
You are lucky indeed if you're hers, my boy;
But there's many a blonde can be equally fond,
If you're only the one she prefers, my boy.

Raven hair or hair of gold,

Devil a bit does it matter I say!
If I love one to-day, why to-morrow I may
Have a caprice for the auburn gay;
So here is a toast to the feminine host,
Blond ringlets for me and the black for you.
The one for a time I shall think sublime,
And then if you like I will change with you.

Harry B. Smith.

HER FAULTS

(From the Mandarin)

MY sweetheart has her faults in plenty,
Which I perceive with much distress;
For instance, she is only twenty,
And one would think her even less;
While I may mention it between us—
(Excuse the confidence betrayed)—
Her form is plagiarized from Venus,
And no acknowledgment is made.

Her hair is much too fine and curly;
Her lips are merely Cupid's bow;
Her teeth absurdly white and pearly;
But still we all have faults, you know.

So, spite of this and spite of that,
Whate'er betide, whate'er befall,
These things let others cavil at;
I love my sweetheart, faults and all.

From such defects this little lady
Of mine is anything but free.
Her lashes are "extremely shady,"
Her eyes are "much too deep for me."
Two dimples have been thought too many
For one small maiden to possess.

Her rivals wish she hadn't any;
But what's a dimple more or less?
Her voice attracts o'er much attention

Because of its melodious ring.
Her foot—but that I shall not mention—
It's such a very little thing.

Yes, spite of that and spite of this,
Whate'er betide, whate'er befall,
Though others may perfection miss,
I love my sweetheart, faults and all.

Harry B. Smith.

A MODERN DIALOGUE

SCENE—*On Manhattan Island. Time—To-day.*
Hour—Ten-thirty. Persons of the play:
SIBYL. *A dream of beauty, half awake,*
In filmy disarray—about to take
Her morning tub. In speech with her the while
Is ROBERT. *He is dressed in riding style.*

SIBYL—Why, Bob, it's *you!* They got your name all wrong.
I'm sorry that I made you wait so long.

BOB—   Only six minutes by my watch—it's true
A minute seems a year, awaiting you!
But Time is merciful and I rejoice
That I am still alive to hear your voice.

SIBYL—A very pretty speech, for you, indeed.
But what extenuation can you plead
For waking ladies at the break of day
From peaceful slumbers, sir!

BOB—   Oh, come, I say!
It's half-past ten!

SIBYL—   Well, it was nearly three
Before I got to bed!

BOB—   Good gracious me!
I'm sure I'd no idea it was so late.
Why, I was riding in the Park at eight
And looked for you. I own I felt abused;
Last night you said——

SIBYL— I beg to be excused
From keeping foolish promises, when made
At two A. M., by moonlight. I'm afraid
My memory's no better than a sieve.
So you expected me? The Lord forgive
Your trusting soul!

BOB— It is His *metier!*

SIBYL—Don't be outrageous, or I'll run away.

BOB— Ah, no; don't go. I will be good, I swear!
'Twas a quotation, Heine, or Voltaire,
Or some fool cynic fellow. By the way,
If you have nothing on, what do you say
To breakfasting with Peg and me at noon
At the Casino?

SIBYL— Well, that's rather soon;
I can't be ready for an hour or more.

BOB— Come as you are, you know that I adore
Your ladyship in any sort of gown;
Besides, there's not another soul in town.
Come as you are; there'll only be we three.

SIBYL—Well, I like that! It's fortunate for me
This is a telephone, and not that new
Invention one can talk and *see* through, too!
What's that you said?

BOB— I didn't speak at all
I only *thought.*

SIBYL— Well, *don't!* Suppose we call

The breakfast half-past one instead of noon?

BOB (*joyously*)—
Then you will come?

SIBYL—　　　　I swear!

BOB—　　　　Not by the moon?

SIBYL (*laughing*)—
No, you may count on me. Now I must fly.
One-thirty—don't forget—Good by!

BOB—　　　　Good by!
(*They ring off.*)

Oliver Herford.

THE POET'S PROPOSAL

"PHYLLIS, if I could I'd paint you
As I see you sitting there,
You distracting little saint, you,
With your aureole of hair.
If I only were an artist,
And such glances could be caught,
You should have the very smartest
Picture frame that can be bought!

"Phyllis, since I can't depict your
Charms, or give you aught but fame,
Will you be yourself the picture?
Will you let me be the frame?
Whose protecting clasp may bind you
Always——"

"Nay," cried Phyllis; "hold,
Or you'll force me to remind you
Paintings must be framed with gold!"

Oliver Herford.

TRUTH

PERMIT me, madame, to declare
That I never will compare
Eyes of yours to Starlight cold,
Or your locks to Sunlight's gold,
Or your lips, I'd have you know,
To the crimson Jacqueminot.

Stuff like that's all very fine
When you get so much a line;
Since I don't, I scorn to tell
Flattering lies. I like too well
Sun and Stars and Jacqueminot
To flatter them, I'd have you know.

Oliver Herford.

THE BACHELOR GIRL

HERE'S to the Bachelor Girl
Who fain her charms would cloister.
She is a precious pearl
That will not leave the oyster.
She is a proud sweet-pea
That scorns to be a vine,
And lean upon a tree
Or round a stick entwine.
"What! lean upon a stick!
Oh, no! I'm not that sort—
I will grow branches thick
And be my own support!"
Beware, O pearl of price,
Lest you be cast to swine;
O proud sweet-pea, think twice
Ere you refuse to twine!
O Bachelor Girl, we drink
Confusion to your plan;
Beware, lest Fate shall link
You to a Spinster Man!

O change, ere 'tis too late,
The Choker tall and silly,
The tweeds—the hat we hate,
For something soft and frilly!
Take off the stockings blue,
(We will avert our gaze),
Then will we drink to you

Long life—and happy days!

Oliver Herford.

THE SEA

SHE was rich, and of high degree;
A poor and unknown artist he.
"Paint me," she said, "a view of the sea."

So he painted the sea as it looked the day
That Aphrodite arose from its spray;
And it broke, as she gazed on its face the while,
Into its countless-dimpled smile.
"What a poky, stupid picture!" said she;
"I don't believe he can paint the sea!"

Then he painted a raging, tossing sea,
Storming, with fierce and sudden shock,
Wild cries, and writhing tongues of foam,
A towering, mighty fastness-rock.
In its sides, above those leaping crests,
The thronging sea-birds built their nests.
"What a disagreeable daub!" said she;
"Why, it isn't anything like the sea!"

Then he painted a stretch of hot, brown sand,
With a big hotel on either hand
And a handsome pavilion for the band—
Not a sign of the water to be seen
Except one faint little streak of green.
"What a perfectly exquisite picture!" said she;
"It's the very image of the sea!"

Eva L. Ogden.

IN PHILISTIA

OF all the places on the map,
Some queer and others queerer,
Arcadia is dear to me,
Philistia is dearer.

There dwell the few who never knew
The pangs of heavenly hunger,
As fresh and fair and fond and frail
As when the world was younger.

If there is any sweeter sound
Than bobolinks or thrushes,
It is the frou-frou of their silks—
The roll of their barouches.

I love them even when they're good,
As well as when they're sinners—
When they are sad and worldly wise
And when they are beginners.

(I say I do; of course the fact,
For better or for worse, is,
My unerratic life denies
My too erotic verses).

I dote upon their waywardness,
Their foibles and their follies.
If there's a madder pate than Di's,
Perhaps it may be Dolly's.

They have no "problems" to discuss,
No "theories" to discover;

They are not "new;" and I—I am
Their very grateful lover.

I care not if their minds confuse
Alastor with Aladdin;
And Cimabue is far less
To them than Chimmie Fadden.

They never heard of William Blake,
Nor saw a Botticelli;
Yet one is, "Yours till death, Louise,"
And one, "Your loving Nelly."

They never tease me for my views,
Nor tax me with my grammar;
Nor test me on the latest news,
Until I have to stammer.

They never talk about their "moods,"
They never know they have them;
The world is good enough for them,
And that is why I love them.

They never puzzle me with Greek,
Nor drive me mad with Ibsen;
Yet over forms as fair as Eve's
They wear the gowns of Gibson.

Bliss Carman.

BETWEEN THE SHOWERS

Between the showers I went my way,
The glistening street was bright with flowers;
It seemed that March had turned to May
Between the showers.

Above the shining roofs and towers
The blue broke forth athwart the gray;
Birds carolled in their leafless bowers.

Hither and thither, swift and gay,
The people chased the changeful hours;
And you, you passed and smiled that day,
Between the showers.

Amy Levy.

GRACE'S CHOICE

When first I saw fair-featured Grace,
In dainty tailor-fashioned gown,
I fell in love with her sweet face,
And pooh-poohed at her escort, Brown.
The fellow's rich, but such a clown!
I did not fear he'd rival me—
I, Reginald de Courcy Drowne,
With wealth and—looks and pedigree.

I set the man a red-hot pace;
It was the talk of all the town;
I knew that I was loved by Grace—
I knew it by that yokel's frown.
My ancestors won great renown,
While Brown has no ancestral tree.
I knew I could the fellow down,
With wealth and—looks and pedigree.

She's married now; has rare point lace,
And jewels fit to deck a crown.
The man who calls her "darling Grace,"
Is not the fellow they call Brown.
No, I'm the happiest man in town.
I knew she'd not say no to me,
One rarely sees Dame Fortune frown
On wealth and—looks and pedigree.

ENVOY

You thought that Grace would marry Brown,
As in most ballades that you see,
But she did not. For her no clown—
But wealth and—looks and pedigree.

Charles Battell Loomis.

TO VIOLET

(With a Bunch of Namesakes)

THERE is a maid—I am afraid
To give her name to you—
Who makes great pets of violets—
I wish I were one, too.

Once in her youth, this all is truth,
She took some up to smell;—
In some strange way the records say,
Into her eyes they fell——

And there they stayed—they never fade—
She looks at me—sometimes,—
And then—Oh, then I seize my pen
And fall to writing rhymes.

But, sad mischance! My consonants
Desert—four vowels, too;
A, E, O, I, take wings, that's why
My rhymes are filled with U.

Robert Cameron Rogers.

HER BONNET

WHEN meeting-bells began to toll,
And pious folk began to pass,
She deftly tied her bonnet on,
The little, sober meeting lass,
All in her neat, white-curtained room, before her tiny looking-glass.

So nicely, round her lady-cheeks,
She smoothed her hands of glossy hair,
And innocently wondered if
Her bonnet did not make her fair—
Then sternly chid her foolish heart for harbouring such fancies there.

So square she tied the satin strings,
And set the bows beneath her chin;
Then smiled to see how sweet she looked;
Then thought her vanity a sin,
And she must put such thoughts away before the sermon should begin.

But, sitting 'neath the prechèd Word,
Demurely in her father's pew,
She thought about her bonnet still,—
Yes, all the parson's sermon through,—
About its pretty bows and buds which better than the text she knew.

Yet sitting there with peaceful face,
The reflex of her simple soul,
She looked to be a very saint—
And maybe was one, on the whole—
Only that her pretty bonnet kept away the aureole.

Mary E. Wilkins.

A SONG

I will not say my true love's eyes
Outshine the noblest star;
But in their depth of lustre lies
My peace, my truce, my war.

I will not say upon her neck
Is white to shame the snow;
For if her bosom hath a speck
I would not have it go.

My love is as a woman sweet,
And as a woman white;
Who's more than this is more than meet
For me and my delight.

Norman R. Gale.

LES PAPILLOTTES

EULALIA sat before the glass
While Betty smoothed her hair.
The mirror told her how she was
Attractive, young and fair;
Curtius was telling her the same
In rosy note, where he confessed his flame.

She read with a satiric eye
Of passion, hope and pain;
Then, careless tossed the poor note by;
Then, took it up again,
And systematically tore,
And folded each strip carefully in four,

And handed in fine scorn each bit
Of rapture to the maid,
Who wot how to dispose of it.
The beauty, disarrayed,
Now crept in bed, blew out the light
Her locks in pink curl-papers for the night.

She slept; and with each gentle breath
The paper in her hair
Soft rustled, and, the story saith,
Repeated to the air
Whate'er stood on it fervent thing—
As if the lover's self were whispering.

And through her dream she heard it say,
The twist o'er her left ear,—

"I vow that I must love alway
The dearest of the dear."
And o'er her forehead spoke a twist,
"That stolen glove I've kissed and over-kissed."

Said one, "Thou are the loveliest;
Thy beauty I adore."
Another, smaller than the rest,
Sighed, "Love, love," o'er and o'er.
And one said, "Pity my sad plight!"
So Curtius' passion pleaded all the night.

Eulalia waking in the morn,
Large-eyed, sat up in bed,
While vows the tend'rest that be sworn
Still whispered in her head;—
A dreamy bliss her soul possessed,—
She rang for Betty; and before she dressed,

Upon a subtly perfumed sheet,
As Curtius' own, blush-pink,
She penned with crow-quill small and neat,
And perfumed crow-black ink,
In flowing hand right tidily,
The proper, simple message, "Come at three."

Gertrude Hall.

UPON GRACIOSA, WALKING AND TALKING

When as abroad, to greet the morn,
I mark my Graciosa walk,
In homage bends the whisp'ring corn,
Yet to confess
Its awkwardness
Must hang its head upon the stalk.

And when she talks, her lips do heal
The wounds her lightest glances give:—
In pity then be harsh, and deal
Such wounds that I
May hourly die,
And, by a word restored, live.

A. Quiller-Couch.

HER VALENTINE

WHAT, send her a valentine? Never!
I see you don't know who "she" is.
I should ruin my chances forever;
My hopes would collapse with a fizz.

I can't see why she scents such disaster
When I take heart to venture a word;
I've no dream of becoming her master,
I've no notion of being her lord.

All I want is to just be her lover!
She's the most up-to-date of her sex,
And there's such a multitude of her,
No wonder they call her complex.

She's a bachelor, even when married,
She's a vagabond, even when housed;
And if ever her citadel's carried
Her suspicions must not be aroused.

She's erratic, impulsive and human,
And she blunders,—as goddesses can;
But if she's what they call the New Woman,
Then I'd like to be the New Man.

I'm glad she makes books and paints pictures,
And typewrites and hoes her own row,
And it's quite beyond reach of conjectures
How much further she's going to go.

When she scorns, in the L-road, my proffer
Of a seat and hangs on to a strap;

I admire her so much, I could offer
To let her ride up on my lap.

Let her undo the stays of the ages,
That have cramped and confined her so long!
Let her burst through the frail candy cages
That fooled her to think they were strong!

She may enter life's wide vagabondage,
She may do without flutter or frill,
She may take off the chains of her bondage,—
And anything else that she will.

She may take me off, for example,
And she probably does when I'm gone.
I'm aware the occasion is ample;
That's why I so often take on.

I'm so glad she can win her own dollars
And know all the freedom it brings.
I love her in shirt-waists and collars,
I love her in dress-reform things.

I love her in bicycle skirtlings—
Especially when there's a breeze—
I love her in crinklings and quirklings
And anything else that you please.

I dote on her even in bloomers—
If Parisian enough in their style—
In fact, she may choose her costumers,
Wherever her fancy beguile.

She may box, she may shoot, she may wrestle,

She may argue, hold office or vote,
She may engineer turret or trestle,
And build a few ships that will float.

She may lecture (all lectures but curtain)
Make money, and naturally spend,
If I let her have her way, I'm certain
She'll let me have mine in the end!

Richard Hovey.

STORY OF THE GATE

ACROSS the pathway, myrtle-fringed,
Under the maple, it was hinged—
The little wooden gate;
'Twas there within the quiet gloam,
When I had strolled with Nelly home,
I used to pause and wait.

Before I said to her good-night,
Yet loath to leave the winsome sprite
Within the garden's pale;
And there, the gate between us two,
We'd linger as all lovers do,
And lean upon the rail.

And face to face, eyes close to eyes,
Hands meeting hands in feigned surprise,
After a stealthy quest,—
So close I'd bend, ere she'd retreat,
That I'd grow drunken from the sweet
Tuberose upon her breast.

We'd talk—in fitful style, I ween—
With many a meaning glance between
The tender words and low;
We'd whisper some dear, sweet conceit,
Some idle gossip we'd repeat,
And then I'd move to go.

"Good-night," I'd say; "Good-night—good-by!"
"Good-night"—from her with half a sigh—

"Good-night!" "Good-night!" And then
And then I do not go, but stand,
Again lean on the railing, and—
Begin it all again.

Ah! that was many a day ago—
That pleasant summer-time—although
The gate is standing yet;
A little cranky, it may be,
A little weather-worn—like me—
Who never can forget.

The happy "End"? My cynic friend,
Pray save your sneers—there was no "end."
Watch yonder chubby thing!
That is our youngest, hers and mine;
See how he climbs, his legs to twine
About the gate and swing.

Harrison Robertson.

TWO TRIOLETS

I
(*What He Said*)

THIS kiss upon your fan I press,

Ah! Saint Nitouche, you don't refuse it,

And may it from its soft recess,

This kiss upon your fan I press,

Be blown to you a shy caress

By this white down whene'er you use it;

This kiss upon your fan I press,

Ah! Saint Nitouche, you don't refuse it.

II
(*What She Thought*)

To kiss a fan!

What a poky poet!

The stupid man

To kiss a fan,

When he knows that—he—can,

Or ought to know it.

To kiss a fan!

What a poky poet!

Harrison Robertson.

A BALLADE OF OLD SWEETHEARTS

WHO is it that weeps for the last year's flowers
When the wood is aflame with the fires of spring,
And we hear her voice in the lilac bowers
As she croons the runes of the blossoming?
For the same old blooms do the new years bring,
But not to our lives do the years come so,
New lips must kiss and new bosoms cling.—
Ah! lost are the loves of the long ago.

Ah me! for a breath of those morning hours
When Alice and I went a-wandering
Through the shining fields, and it still was ours
To kiss and to feel we were shuddering—
Ah me! when a kiss was a holy thing—
How sweet were a smile from Maud, and oh!
With Phyllis once more to be whispering—
Ah! lost are the loves of the long ago.

But it cannot be that old Time devours
Such loves as was Annie's and mine we sing,
And surely beneficent heavenly powers
Save Muriel's beauty from perishing;
And if in some golden evening
To a quaint old garden I chance to go,
Shall Marion no more by the wicket sing?—
Ah! lost are the loves of the long ago.

L'ENVOI

In these lives of ours do the new years bring
Old loves as old flowers again to blow?
Or do new lips kiss and new bosoms cling?—
Ah! lost are the loves of the long ago.

Richard Le Gallienne.

AMOUR DE VOYAGE

AND I was a man who could write you rhyme
(Just so much for you, nothing more),
And you were the woman I loved for a time—
Loved for a little, and nothing more,
We shall go our ways when the voyage is o'er,
You with your beauty and I with my rhymes,
With a dim remembrance rising at times
(Only a memory, nothing more)
Of a lovely face and some worthless rhymes.

Meantime till our comedy reaches its end
(It's comic ending, and nothing more)
I shall live as your lover who loved as a friend—
Shall swear true love till Life be o'er.
And you, you must make believe and attend,
As the steamer throbs from shore to shore.

And so, we shall pass the time for a little
(Pass it in pleasure, and nothing more),
For vows, alas! are sadly brittle,
And each may forget the oaths that we swore.
And have we not loved for an age, and age?
And was I not yours from shore to shore?
From landing-stage to landing-stage
Did I not worship and kneel and adore?
And what is a month in love but an age?
And who in their senses would wish for more?

Rudyard Kipling.

THE LOVERS' LITANY

EYES of gray—a sodden quay,
Driving rain and falling tears,
As the steamer wears to sea
In a parting storm of cheers.
Sing, for Faith and Hope are high—
None so true as you and I—
Sing the Lovers' Litany:—
"Love like ours can never die!"

Eyes of black—a throbbing keel,
Milky foam to left and right;
Whispered converse near the wheel
In the brilliant tropic night.
Cross that rules the Southern Sky!
Stars that sweep and wheel and fly
Hear the Lovers' Litany:—
"Love like ours can never die!"

Eyes of brown—a dusty plain
Split and parched with heat of June,
Flying hoof and tightened rein,
Hearts that beat the old old tune.
Side by side the horses fly,
Frame we now the old reply
Of the Lovers' Litany:—
"Love like ours can never die!"

Eyes of blue—the Simla Hills
Silvered with the moonlight hoar;
Pleading of the waltz that thrills,

Dies and echoes round Benmore.
"*Mabel*," "*Officers*," "*Good-by*,"
Glamour, wine, and witchery—
On my soul's sincerity,
"*Love like ours can never die!*"

Maidens, of your charity,
Pity my most luckless state.
Four times Cupid's debtor I—
Bankrupt in quadruplicate.
Yet, despite this evil case,
And a maiden showed me grace,
Four-and-forty times would I
Sing the Lovers' Litany:—
"*Love like ours can never die!*"

Rudyard Kipling.

A LENTEN CALL

'TWAS the second of March, in the present year,
And the morning after a revel,
When the world and the flesh made a party call,
Accompanied by the Devil.

Their coats were creaseless, their "patents" shone,
And the Devil smiled most sweetly,
To think that a carefully built-up shoe,
Hid his cloven hoof completely.

They rang the bell at Society's door,
Sent in their names and stood waiting,
The usual warm reception there
Serenely anticipating.

But the white-capped maid returned and said
In a voice demurely level,
That her mistress was not at home that day
To the World, the Flesh or the Devil.

The World and the Flesh grew pale—as well
They might do, with propriety—
For they'd be in a parlous state, without
The countenance of Society.

And even the Devil looked half-perplexed
Till he cried—"Ah! I see the reason!
It is one of Society's yearly fads,
And this is the Lenten season."

Then they all three laughed, both loud and long,
For it certainly did relieve them

To think that after some forty days
Society would receive them;

And that the unwonted quiet would give
New zest to each after-revel,
When Society opened her doors again
To the World, the Flesh and the Devil.

Hilda Johnson Wise.

HELEN'S FACE A BOOK

HELEN'S face is like a book—
Charming, all its pages.
Helen's face is like a book;
What's the story I forsook,
When on Helen's face I look,
When her smile engages?

There I read an old romance;
Here, I see one living!
There, I read an old romance,
But in Helen's lightest glance
Far a livelier tale enchants,
Wild excitement giving!

What is printer's ink to me?
Commas, dots and dashes!
What is printer's ink to me,
If with Helen I may be,
Exclamation points to see
Underneath her lashes?

Gelett Burgess.

THE BUTTERFLY'S MADRIGAL

LOVE-for-a-day, come let's be gay!

Love, for a day, thy lips are smiling!

Love-for-a-week, our bliss we'll seek,

Love, for a week, dull care beguiling!

Love-for-a-year, be true my dear!

Love, for a year—and then we'll sever;

Love for a day or year we may,

But Love for aye—ah, never!

Gelett Burgess.

BALLADE OF THE DEVIL-MAY-CARE

FREE as the wandering pike am I,
Many the strings to my amorous bow,
More than a little inclined to fly
Butterfly lovering, to and fro;
Happy wherever the flowers blow,
With the dew on the leaf, and the sunshine above,
Terribly wrong and unprincipled? No,
Life is too short to be "dead in love!"

Not for me is the lover's sigh;
Fools are they to be worrying so!
Sipping my fill of the honey I fly
Butterfly lovering, to and fro.
I skim the cream, and let all else go;
Gather my roses, and give a shove
Over my shoulder at dutiful woe,—
Life is too short to be "dead in love!"

So, while the fanciful hours go by,
I gayly reap what the simpletons sow.
Fresh with their bloom are the fruits I try,
Butterfly lovering, to and fro.
Then here's to the lady who wears her beau
On and off, like a dainty glove!
And here's to the zephyrs that all-ways blow—
Life is too short to be "dead in love!"

ENVOY

Prince, who cares for the coming snow,

Butterfly lovering to and fro?
Why should a man be a turtle-dove?
Life is too short to be "dead in love!"
Gelett Burgess.

BALLADE OF DREAMS TRANSPOSED

SOME may like to be shut in a cage,
Cooped in a corner, a-tippling tea,
Some may in troublesome toil engage;
But the luck of a rover's the thing for me!
Over the mountain and over the sea,
Now in the country and now in the town,
And when I'm wrinkled and withered, maybe,
Then I'll marry and settle down.

Some may pore over printed page
And never know bird, nor beast, nor tree,
Watching the world from book or stage;
But the luck of a rover's the thing for me!
So ho! for the forest, and ho! for the lea,
And ho! for the river and prairie brown,
And ho! for a gay long jubilee,—
Then I'll marry and settle down.

Why should I wait till a gray old age
Brings me chance to be rich and free?
I have no money—it makes me rage;
But the luck of a rover's the thing for me!
Though oft, with my lover upon my knee
(She has frolicsome eyes and a fetching gown!)
I fear if my heart's to be held in fee,—
Then I'll marry and settle down.

ENVOY

Prince, my sweetheart will not agree,—
But the luck of a rover's the thing for me!
She says I must stay, and I fear her frown,—
Then I'll marry and settle down.

Gelett Burgess.

VILLANELLE OF HIS LADY'S TREASURE

I TOOK her dainty eyes, as well
As silken tendrils of her hair:
And so I made a Villanelle!

I took her voice, a silver bell,
As clear as song, as soft as prayer;
I took her dainty eyes as well.

It may be, said I, who can tell,
These things shall be my less despair?
And so I made a Villanelle!

I took her whiteness virginal
And from her cheek two roses rare:
I took her dainty eyes as well.

I said: "It may be possible
Her image from my heart to tear!"
And so I made a Villanelle.

I stole her laugh, most musical:
I wrought it in with artful care;
I took her dainty eyes as well;
And so I made a Villanelle.

Ernest Dowson.

L'ENVOI

GO, pretty Rose, and to her tell
All I would say, could I but see
The slender form I know so well,
The roguish eyes that laughed at me.

And when your fragrance fills the room,
Tell her of all I hope and fear;
With every breath of sweet perfume,
Whisper my greetings in her ear.

But, Roses, stay—there is one thing
You must not mention (don't forget,
For it might be embarrassing),
And that is, you're not paid for yet!

E. B. Reed.

A MERRY BLUE-EYED LADDIE

A MERRY blue-eyed laddie goes laughing through the town,
Singing, "Hey, but the world is a gay, gay, place!"
And every little lassie smooths her tumbled locks a-down,
And brings out all her dimples and hides away her frown,
And lays aside her broom and mop, the bonnie boy to chase,
Singing, "Hey, but the world is a gay, gay place!"

But away the blue-eyed laddie goes to seek another town,
Singing, "Hey, but the world is a gay, gay place!"
Then every dimple vanishes, and back comes every frown,
And every little lassie folds away her Sunday gown,
With tear-drops trickling sadly down her woful little face,
Sighing, "Hey, but the world is a sad, sad place!"

Juliet Wilbour Tompkins.

DANCE TIME

IT'S I live in a very wise town
As all wise people know:
They read, they write, they read all day
As orchard-trees do grow.

Said I,—I was a young thing then,
And a foolish young thing, too,—
"I will not spend my little life thus;
There's much I'd rather do.

"For I would rather look at you
This way, with happy looks,
Than lose the stars from my two eyes
With poring over books.

"I'd rather far be red and white
For stupid folks to see
Than write nine books for little dull worms
To eat them, leisurely.

"And I would rather have it said
When all my days are through,
'O she was good to see and hear
And say Good-morning to!'

"When learning makes you white and red
And fresh as west-winds blow,
I may spend sun and candle-light
To learn what they all know.

"But O, the wise in this wise town,
They have no longer prime.

And there are fewer wise men, now,
Than once upon a time!"

Josephine Preston Peabody Marks.

HOW LIKE A WOMAN

I WANTED you to come to-day—
Or so I told you in my letter—
And yet, if you had stayed away,
I should have liked you so much better.
I should have sipped my tea unseen,
And thrilled at every door-bell's pealing,
And thought how nice I could have been
Had you evinced a little feeling.

I should have guessed you drinking tea
With someone whom you loved to madness;
I should have thought you cold to me,
And revelled in a depth of sadness.
But, no! you came without delay—
I could not feel myself neglected:
You said the things you always say,
In ways not wholly unexpected.

If you had let me wait in vain,
We should, in my imagination,
Have held, what we did not attain,
A most dramatic conversation.
Had you not come, I should have known
At least a vague anticipation,
Instead of which, I grieve to own,
You did not give me one sensation.

Caroline and Alice Duer.

A VIGNETTE

CUPID, playing blind man's buff,

Seized my Psyche's floating tresses.

Here is silken clue enough

To dispense with any guesses.

This is Psyche's golden fleece:

She's my prisoner, past release.

But the lookers-on declare

Love was caught in Psyche's hair.

Caroline Duer.

Milton Keynes UK
Ingram Content Group UK Ltd.
UKHW020831231024
450026UK00005B/509